The Recent History
of the United States
in Political Cartoons

The Recent History
of the United States
in Political Cartoons

A Look Bok!

Chip Bok

Forewords by John C. Green and Dave Barry

**The University of
Akron Press**
Akron, Ohio

All inquiries and permissions requests should be addressed to the

publisher, The University of Akron Press, Akron, OH 44325–1703

Manufactured in the United States of America

First edition 2005

09   08   07   06   05   5   4   3   2   1

Library of Congress Cataloging-in-Publication Data

Bok, Chip, 1952-
    The recent history of the United States in political cartoons : a look
Bok! / Chip Bok.—1st ed.
        p. cm.—(Series on law, politics, and society)
    ISBN 1-931968-11-X (cloth : alk. paper)—ISBN 1-931968-12-8
    (pbk. : alk. paper)
    1. United States—Politics and government—1945-1989—Caricatures
and cartoons. 2. United States—Politics and government—1989—
Caricatures and cartoons. 3. United States—Social conditions—1960-
1980—Caricatures and cartoons. 4. United States—Social
conditions—1980—Caricatures and cartoons. 5. Political cartoons—
United States. 6. Editorial cartoons—United States. 7. Wit and humor,
Pictorial. 8. Bok, Chip, 1952-   9. Editorial cartoonists—United States—
Biography. I. Title. II. Series.

E839.5B64 2005
973.92'02'07—dc22   2005041935

The paper used in this publication meets the minimum requirements of

American National Standard for Information Sciences—Permanence of

Paper for Printed Library Materials, ANSI Z39.48—1984. ∞

Contents

Forewords

I read newspapers as part of my job. My day begins with the papers at the breakfast table and afterward online. I review the news, skim the pundits, and peruse the editorials.

Then I turn to a guilty pleasure: political cartoons.

Every morning, I *need* to know what is happening and what is being said about it, but I *want* to know who is being laughed at.

For almost two decades, the guiltiest of these pleasures has been the editorial cartoons by Chip Bok in my hometown newspaper, the *Akron Beacon Journal.*

People often ask me: how can you keep your composure, let alone your sanity, when you follow politics so closely?

Well, I have a deep and abiding love for American political institutions, a great appreciation for the spectacle of a free people governing themselves, and a wicked sense of humor.

Chip Bok and his cartooning brethren are essential to maintaining the latter.

I have a special fondness for Bok in part because his career parallels my own. The cartoons in this volume begin with Richard Nixon and cover the presidencies of Gerald Ford, Jimmy Carter, Ronald Reagan, George H. Bush, Bill Clinton, and George W. Bush. These are the presidents I have tried to understand.

Bok also is a pal of my favorite humorist, Dave Barry. Barry has documented some of Bok's more interesting escapades in his columns (and claims he is not making this up). Bok illustrated some of Barry's work, so Barry may have gotten the better part of the bargain.

Bok and Barry have helped me through some amazing and trying times. So, I'm pleased that he has followed Barry's lead and reprinted his best work in book form.

Politics can be usefully thought of as a conversation—a sprawling, brawling conversation with many and varied voices. Some give official pronouncements, others spread the daily gossip, and still others earnestly seek the truth. Cartoonists are in the peanut gallery, making witty asides and heckling those on stage.

These jokesters relieve the tension when the talk gets hot and stir things up when it gets dull. They tell us when we should be outraged and when we should let matters slide. They puncture the pompous, lambaste the liars, and mince the mighty.

In short, they give us perspective on the conversation.

They are credible in this regard because they are part of the conversation too, with the same foibles and limitations as everyone else. They don't rise above the din, but instead cut through it, with willful exaggeration and little flecks of truth.

Laughter is a very democratic thing. If nothing else, everyone and anyone can laugh at the foolish parts of the conversation. And such laughter communicates something rather profound: in the end, no one is in charge of life, liberty, and everything else except us.

So humor is about serious business, and the more serious the business, the more important humor becomes.

Here political cartoonists offer something special because their medium is visual. Caricature, whimsy, and absurd drawings illuminate the conversation in both familiar and surprising ways. Ordinary matters become potent symbols of our collective experience.

It is no accident that some of the most enduring symbols of American politics came from cartoonists, the Republican elephant and Democratic donkey being the best known. Surely the symbols of the next era are being drawn today—and a prescient reader might even find some hints of them in these pages.

In fact, we know our presidents as much from their cartoons as from their official portraits—such as Richard Nixon's paranoid jowls and Bill Clinton's philandering smile. Of course, the best cartoons are portraits—portraits of our intimate knowledge of these leaders. They are especially relevant in the age of television and the Internet, when reality is often a bit less than real.

Chip Bok is an adept practitioner of this craft. His enthusiastic participation in the conversation for about thirty years is chronicled in these pages. A useful commentary accompanies the cartoons, just in case the reader needs a reminder of the discussion. But by and large, the cartoons speak for themselves. They are brash, fierce, clever, insightful, and, well, funny.

These cartoons occurred in the context of a tumultuous conversation. The era—our era—began with the 1964 presidential election. Lyndon Johnson's landslide victory over Barry Goldwater marked both the high point and unraveling of the political order that had governed the country since the 1930s.

On a positive note, real progress was made on civil and women's rights, and the United States won the Cold War. On a negative note, the nation was bedeviled by grinding conflict, including five one-term presidents, four significant minor party revolts, the first president to resign and only the second to be impeached—not to mention one of the closest and most controversial elections ever. Bok supplied a lot of perspective during these interesting times.

My favorite cartoon in this collection is found near the end of this era. It shows Chief Wahoo, the controversial mascot of the Cleveland Indians, on stage at President Clinton's first "conversation on race," held in Akron, Ohio. An angry president is shouting, "Who let him in?"

I was in the audience at that event and remember seeing the cartoon in the newspaper. It certainly unsettled me, but it also made me laugh because of its fair comment. Bok received a reprimand from his editors for his part in this conversation. It's not all fun in the peanut gallery.

Like many of his colleagues, Bok has developed skepticism to a high art. But I see little cynicism in these drawings. Behind his wicked sense of humor, one can sense a deep and abiding love for American political institutions as well as a great appreciation for the spectacle of a free people governing themselves.

And as Dave Barry might say, I'm not making this up.

John C. Green

When you were in junior high, you probably had one classmate who really, really liked to draw cartoons. He—it's almost always a boy—was a little weird, but semi-popular with the other boys, because his drawings were funny and often depicted people naked. He was smart, but he didn't get particularly good grades, because he was more interested in drawing cartoons than in studying. Sometimes the teacher would chastise him for wasting his talent; he would respond by drawing a cartoon of the teacher naked.

Have you ever wondered what happened to that classmate? I can tell you: He became chairman of the Federal Reserve Board.

No, seriously, he probably at least tried to make a living as a cartoonist, and if he was truly talented and dedicated—but did not mature too much—he ended up working as a newspaper editorial cartoonist. And now, instead of drawing naked people, the weird kid is using his pen to make public fun of the most powerful politicians in the world.

As a humor columnist, I also work in the whoopee-cushion sector of journalism. So over the years, I've come to know many cartoonists, and one of my favorites, as both a professional and a guy, is Chip Bok. I met him in the early 1980s in Miami, where both he and I worked for the *Miami Herald*'s wonderful (and, alas, now defunct) Sunday magazine, *Tropic*. For a while, Chip drew terrific illustrations for my column, but before long his talent took him to the *Akron Beacon Journal*, for whom he has been turning out wonderful work ever since.

But I don't only follow Chip's career from afar. I also join forces with him every four years at the Democratic and Republican conventions, where he and I, and often other cartoonists, form ourselves into an informal, but also highly disorganized, Humor Patrol, prowling the convention hall and the host city in search of things to make fun of. This mission often entails crashing lavish, corporate-sponsored parties and consuming free food and drink (hey, somebody has to do it). I have found that, in these situations, there is nobody I can count on for an entertaining evening more than I count on Chip Bok.

For example, at the 2000 Democratic convention in Los Angeles, Chip and I and maybe a half-dozen other cartoonists got into a very exclusive party by somehow persuading the city's then-mayor, Dick Riordan, to let us act as his security detail. We gave ourselves secret code names, such as Kitchen Magician, Pocket Fisherman, and Eggplant. We wore dark suits and sunglasses, although it was night. For radio communication, we removed the cords from our hotel telephones, sticking one end into our ears, and the other into our suit pockets; this did not actually enable us to communicate, but it did look really, really stupid.

When we arrived at the party, we formed a clot around the mayor and whisked right past the bouncers. Once inside, we abandoned the mayor and went to the bar; our dedication to duty only went so far.

My last clear memory of that party is an image of Chip Bok: He was leaning against the bar, surveying the scene. He still had his sunglasses on. He'd tried to remove the phone cord from his ear, but it was stuck, so it was still lodged in there, with the free end now swinging loose in the breeze. There he stood, surveying the scene, gathering material, phone cord dangling from his ear: A cartoonist in action. You have to love this man.

Dave Barry

Introduction

E ditorial cartoonists lurk in the back alleys of respectable journalism. We loiter there waiting to pick off passing politicians. It is rewarding work. Witnesses to the job are the readers, bystanders who watch a mugging performed for their amusement. Sometimes they are appalled and call the cops (my editor). Other times they cheer me on like a mob yelling "Jump!" In the worst case, they ignore me.

More than once my former editor, Dave Cooper, referred to this audience as "the Poor Reader." As he navigated some mental obstacle course I had constructed, he would say, "You're making it awfully hard on the poor reader." That is where the "seven second" rule comes in. It is the amount of time I have before the Poor Reader's attention wanders off to something more meaningful, like the underwear ads.

Like so much back alley work today, editorial cartooning doesn't seem to have much of a future. Only about 150 editorial cartoonists are working full-time today, and probably fewer will be tomorrow. Syndicated cartoons are cheaper and easier to deal with than a live, breathing, and eating staff cartoonist. They arrive from the syndicate electronically, require no health care or benefits, and don't argue with the editor.

As an endangered industry, political cartooning seeks, and gets, federal protection. It comes in the form of the First Amendment to the U.S. Constitution. This protection was made ironclad thanks to pornographer and patron saint of cartoonists Larry Flynt. He was sued by Rev. Jerry Falwell over the emotional distress caused by a cartoon that appeared in Flynt's magazine, *Hustler*, in 1983. The cartoon played off a series of Campari Liqueur ads that asked, "When was your first time?" The landmark image depicted Rev. Falwell having sex, for the first time, with his mother in an outhouse. Everybody agrees the cartoon was raunchy, in bad taste, and based on no fact whatsoever—just what the First Amendment was designed for, according to the U.S. Supreme Court. In its 1988 majority opinion, written by Chief Justice William Rehnquist in favor of Larry Flynt, the Court said, "The appeal of the political cartoon or caricature is often based on exploration of unfortunate physical traits or politically embarrassing events . . . often calculated to hurt the feelings of the subject of the portrayal." In order to protect political cartoons, the court protected Larry Flynt's offensive cartoon. Not many jobs have a Supreme Court mandate to cause emotional distress.

Maybe being Larry Flynt's godchildren has something to do with the declining number of editorial cartoonists these days. While the death of newspapers has been exaggerated, they do face stiff competition from BlackBerrys, blogs, iPods, laptops, Handsprings, XM radio, shock jocks, and Comedy Central. Most young people don't read newspapers on a daily basis, and even aging baby boomers don't always have a daily paper delivered at home. Faced with these odds, and considering the big bucks the entertainment industry pays for bad taste these days, you might think the print industry would embrace its court-certified cartoonists. But you would be wrong.

Nineteenth-century editorial cartoonist Thomas Nast drew Irishmen like monkeys and Catholic clergy like crocodiles. It's hard to imagine today's sensitive media leaders running wild with portrayals of "unfortunate physical traits or politically embarrassing events." They don't object to portraying politically embarrassing events—as long as those events are politically incorrect, like the Abu Ghraib prison scandal in Iraq. Issues blessed by the mainstream media, like the environment or sexual orientation, aren't so likely to be ridiculed. Cartoons that take a skeptical view of global warming, for example, seldom appear in the pages of *Newsweek* or *USA Today*. Readers notice this lack of uniform skepticism, and consider it a credibility issue. We've reached a point where hurtful speech is banned in the workplace and universities but encouraged on the editorial page by the U.S. Supreme Court. You'd think there would be a stronger market for cartoons, wouldn't you?

I have been exploring unfortunate physical traits and politically embarrassing events for the past twenty-five years. I thought it might be interesting to look back at them as a cartoon history loosely built around presidents from Nixon forward. Many history books use cartoons to illustrate the text, but this one will use text to illustrate the cartoons.

One thing that became apparent, as I began assembling cartoons, was that some hot current issues in the news are actually recurring themes. Everybody is shocked by the release of photographs of what went on in Iraq's Abu Ghraib prison. As I write this (early June 2004), telephone transcripts from the National Archive have revealed Henry Kissinger's attempt to prevent the release of the 1968 My Lai massacre photos.

I sifted through more than four thousand cartoons with the help of Michael J. Carley and Amy Freels Petersen of the University of Akron Press. From a selection of about three hundred of them, a picture emerged of life and politics over the last twenty-five years, at least the way I saw it. Also interesting was how my career had evolved during those years. Ask Al Gore: nothing ever goes the way you expect.

It's not easy to get started as a cartoonist. The great *Dayton Daily News* cartoonist Mike Peters helped me launch my career, but it still took me six years after college to land my first job at the *Clearwater Sun* in Florida. Their new editor, Ray Jenkins, hired me as their first editorial cartoonist. Six months and a management change later, I was fired. The new editor, John Perry, initially allowed me to stay, but insisted that I draw only local cartoons. Apparently it didn't take me long to offend most of the people he wanted to impress.

Here are some cartoons that were in the paper. Clearwater and Pinellas County were a bit removed from what could actually be considered the South in cultural terms. There were, however, elements of the Old South present, including the Ku Klux Klan. Another pest, the medfly, had been found in the state. (The medfly was cause for concern because it attacks the citrus crop. The only thing more damaging to the Florida economy would be if medflies were eating sales tax–paying

tourists.) California had some success in dealing with the medfly by introducing sterile males into the population. I wondered if this remedy might work with the Ku Klux Klan population.

Elements of the Klan were closer than I knew. I dropped my cartoon off at engraving and went home for the day. The next morning I was miffed to open the paper and not find it on the editorial page. Editor Ray Jenkins just said, "Looks like we've been sabotaged. You'll have to put the same one in again today." I began to realize that people paid attention to my cartoons.

When one of the candidates for the Largo City Commission was found sitting in his driveway stacking and unstacking dimes, I took the opportunity to poke fun at the commission. The cutline to my cartoon read, "Awright awright, so I'm not insane. I still have other qualifications for the Largo Commission." It didn't seem so funny when he committed suicide the next week. Local cartoons are tough.

Pinellas County had a mix of the petty and the bizarre. The landmark Harrison Hotel in Clearwater had been secretly purchased as a headquarters by the Scientologists. A group was formed to oppose Scientology, but wanted its membership to be secret to avoid retribution. Scientology beat reporter Rich Leiby told me he had seen classified Scientology papers claiming that the human race was descended from Thetons, spirits of beings from the planet Xemu. This was heady stuff in a community with a very large retirement population, many soon to become spirits themselves.

In other big stories, the Largo police conducted an undercover surveillance operation of a garage poker game regularly attended by eight retired guys who became known as the Largo 8. A three-legged dog with a bowling ball tied to its neck was found on the rocks in Tampa Bay near the causeway and became a causeway célèbre. Against this backdrop, a Salvador Dali museum was constructed in neighboring St. Petersburg.

The morning my Dali cartoon appeared, John Perry called me into his office to explain that freedom of the press is a right that applies only to those who own a

"SURREALISM IMPROBABLE IN PINELLAS COUNTY? OH, I DON'T KNOW ABOUT THAT."

press. Then he fired me. It didn't have anything to do with any particular cartoon, he said, he just "didn't like any" of my cartoons. I should have unleashed Larry Flynt on him.

It was a tough time to be out of a job. A severe recession set in with the beginning of the Reagan administration. My wife Deb and I had married right after college and, amazingly, we were still married with a year-old son. I was too embarrassed to tell my parents that, after spending six years to find my first job, it took me only six months to lose it. When they came to visit from Ohio I would leave in the morning, go to the library to scout newspaper addresses, and come back in the afternoon.

I did freelance work for *South Florida Magazine* in Miami, the *Miami Herald*, the *St. Petersburg Times,* and *Tampa Magazine.* I also talked Bud Faulder, the news director at the ABC affiliate in Tampa, into letting me use the station's weather computer to create animations. Oh, yeah. I drew caricatures at Busch Gardens in Tampa, too. What I didn't realize was that everything I was doing would pay off down the road.

I began illustrating a newspaper column by a funny guy named Dave Barry at the *Miami Herald*'s Sunday magazine, *Tropic.* Knight Ridder, the *Herald*'s parent company, was developing new videotex technology, and I used one of my weather computer animations to land a job with this upstart in a dubious new field. Viewtron, one of the country's first online services, was launched, and so was my new career. It was fun to live in Miami—and even more fun to get a regular paycheck. The next time my parents visited, I took them on a tour of Viewtron.

I kept my freelance work with *South Florida* and *Tropic* and also began drawing a weekly business cartoon for *Miami Review.* Gene Weingarten, *Tropic*'s editor, agreed to give me my own weekly cartoon, which we imaginatively titled: "BOK." It was about South Florida stuff: cinch bugs, strangler figs, alligators, and cockroaches big enough to compete for dock space at Chalk Airlines, the Biscayne Bay float plane service to the Bahamas. One cartoon drew undue attention to Miami's crime problem, and Weingarten received a memo from the *Herald*'s managing editor, Heath Merriweather. The memo said, "Bok's cartoons suck. That means I don't like them. That means get rid of him." Other managers intervened on my behalf, and I avoided the axe.

I began to realize that Mike Peters had neglected to mention one minor detail to me as he prepped me for my cartoon career. I did not draw very well. That's like being a catcher without a mitt or a pilot with a fear of heights. I was usually the best drawer in my class, but the best ball player in the neighborhood doesn't just go off and make the pros. Don Wright, the two-time Pulitzer-winning cartoonist at the *Miami News*, helped me focus on the need to draw something that looked more like what editorial page editors were expecting. The Poor Reader, I learned, was not

alone in the misery I was inflicting. There was now also the Poor Editor. This new insight, along with the actual seeing skills I developed while drawing speedy caricatures at Busch Gardens, had me ready to take another crack at editorial cartoons. That was a good thing, because Knight-Ridder, after spending millions of dollars convincing itself that videotex would not annihilate its newspaper business, shut down the Viewtron project, and I was out of a job again. By that time, however, my *Tropic* cartoon was gaining in popularity, and I had several offers. I moved to Knight Ridder's *Akron Beacon Journal*, John S. Knight's original paper.

John S. Knight left behind a legacy of independence. The main conference room at the paper, The John S. Knight Room, is a shrine to the great man. Many of his sayings adorn the walls, including: "I'm not afraid of anybody." "There is no greater title than editor." "I cling to the old-fashioned view that editors are supposed to have opinions, so I express them." And "I know what I know." He was known for encouraging his papers to find the truth and print it. This was true even when it harmed his own interests. The *Herald* crusaded against illegal gambling joints in the Miami area, even though Mr. Knight was one of their best customers.

Happily, this kind of journalistic independence continued into my own era. In 1994, Sun TV and Appliance in Akron sold some computers that came with an unexpected bonus. The computers evidently were "preowned" and, to their new owners' surprise, they came preloaded with pornographic software. The *Beacon Journal* ran the story and I drew a cartoon.

The president of Sun TV was not amused and, as a major advertiser, summoned my publisher, John Dotson, to his office. (This is worse than calling the cops.) With the newspaper spread on his desk, he pointed to the cartoon and demanded to know what the publisher thought of it. "I think it's funny," was the reply that cost a million dollars in advertising. It was an honest answer to a question about a cartoon based on an honest story. The advertising eventually came back. The value of the integrity John Dotson showed was paid back in the willingness of people to read our paper and trust it.

Things have not changed under Jim Crutchfield, Dotson's successor. All this is a good deal for me. I'm glad I don't have have to grovel or flatter our editorial page editor, Mike Douglas, a witty and handsome man who is kind to animals and small children, admired by men, and adored by women. A gifted athlete and renaissance man who towers over his peers, Mr. Douglas is far too large a figure to trifle with a cartoon that runs counter to his own profound and erudite opinions.

Soon after my arrival in Akron I learned that Ohio's politics are as interesting as Florida's. Some cronies of Ohio Supreme Court Justice Craig Wright had a case before the high court in 1991. Justice Wright had gone on a Florida golf junket with these friends, the *Beacon Journal* broke the story, and I drew a cartoon.

Justice Wright became enraged when fellow justice Andy Douglas needled him about the cartoon. Things escalated, and the two came to blows and wrestled to the floor in chambers. I think William Rehnquist would rule that an image that causes a fist fight between Supreme Court justices is the ultimate definition of cartoon success. It is rewarding work.

Richard M. Nixon, the 37th president of the United States, alias: Tricky Dick, Milhouse 1

CHAPTER 1

The Nixon, Ford, and Carter Years

My cartoon record is sparse throughout the Nixon, Ford, and Carter administrations. That's unfortunate, because it was a great time of stumbles, head bumps, WIN (Whip Inflation Now) buttons, national malaise, cardigan sweaters, and attack rabbits. It was a time of frustration, humiliation, and anger. Things weren't going so well in politics or government, either.

After bracing days spent raking concrete for the Baker Cement company in the late '70s, I would retire in the evenings to my makeshift home studio and fall asleep. If I stayed awake I tried to draw cartoons to add to my meager portfolio, with the hope of eventually occupying one of the 150 or so editorial cartoon jobs in existence at the time. It was a strange ambition, and the odds were not good. The Nixon, Ford, Carter procession provoked an unfocused anger in me that I raised to the level of passion in my own mind. I was shocked—shocked—to learn that presidents lie. I was even more distressed to learn that sometimes they sought the presidency just to be president. The idea of seeking the presidency for its own sake was upsetting to my developing sense of high purpose. It was an insight I needed to share visually, via ripping humor, with my fellow man—at the proper compensation level with full benefits, of course. Like an overlooked Paul Revere, or terrorism czar Richard Clarke, I felt I would have failed the American people if I didn't warn them that presidents lie.

My anger may have been fuzzy, but my intentions were sharply focused on any one of those 150 jobs. The only thing standing between my urgent message and my future readers (and paychecks) were editors. The cowards didn't have the *cojones* to see that their current cartoonists, unaware that presidents lie, were in need of immediate replacement by me. I would even have thrown in the information that presidents are power hungry, at no additional charge.

This failure of the press caused me to continue drawing portfolio cartoons after my next job as a substitute teacher and my next job after that as a wholesale drug salesman. The abdication of journalistic responsibility by those with the power to hire would linger, like a stain from a rapidograph pen left open in an unprotected shirt pocket, until the end of the Carter administration. No wonder there had been national malaise.

Without a cartoonist to tell the people that their rulers lie, there were only rabbits left to attack presidents. And that is precisely what happened. President Jimmy Carter was blindsided by an attack rabbit while he fished. Apparently, no Secret Service agent lunged forward to take the rabbit for him. The renegade rodent was eventually subdued and the entire incident hushed up. I believe the bunny's body is being secretly kept in Area 51 near Roswell, New Mexico. I have no published cartoon to document this disturbing incident, due to the disgraceful six-year media conspiracy to hush me up.

James Earl Carter, the 39th president of the United States, alias: Jimmy

Also missing from the record are published cartoons of President Ford's headfirst encounter with an airplane door, Arab sheikhs causing honest Americans to sit strapped into Pintos and Vegas in long gas lines, or any whimsical iconography of the Ayatollah Khomeni.

Gerald R. Ford, the 38th president of the United States, alias: Gerald Ford

ADOPT A CARTOONIST

THIS IS CHIP (on the left). Like thousands of other artists he needs a home. Amazingly, little Chip here has managed to survive on nuts, berries and rare bits of edible freelance work since the ruthless abandonment by his family at the age of 24. He's friendly, doesn't eat much and he's housebroken.

When the force of my arguments and whining failed to land me on the editorial page of a metropolitan daily, I changed course and bid for pity. This is the cover of a brochure I mailed around the country. Of course the attempt to elicit pity didn't work either. We are talking about newspaper editors.

I did manage to publish a few freelance cartoons at the *Kettering Oakwood Times* in Ohio during the '70s, and I drew some others for various college newspapers. This is the first editorial cartoon I ever had published. It appeared in the *Kettering Oakwood Times* and is a meditation on the irrepressible spirit of FBI director J. Edgar Hoover, who died May 2, 1972. I think he's looking for something sassy, yet somber, to wear.

The stuffy manners of our parents' world were overthrown during the late '60s and early '70s. But a new etiquette filled the vacuum. It became acceptable to use profanity in the presence of a woman but unacceptable to refer to her as a girl. The old rules were replaced with new rules—it was just a bit dicey figuring out what they were. A new polite behavior, version 2.0, soon evolved into full-blown political correctness. Opening doors and letting ladies go first became a case-by-case proposition. Fat folk, as objects of ridicule, had not yet been taken off the table.

Being educated, in the early '70s I considered myself to be liberal—like everyone else I knew. However, there was quite a bit of dogma that elite liberals preached more than they practiced. I enjoyed tweaking them for it.

In 1974, U.S. District Judge Arthur Garrity Jr. ordered the Boston schools to be integrated by busing children from white neighborhoods to schools in black neighborhoods and vice versa. It was a popular move with liberals whose children attended private schools, but parents in white South Boston were not so keen on the practice. Violence was shown on TV news every night as kids were shipped off to school in the morning. Judges, being judges, began ordering busing in cities all over the country.

The same theme pops up in school voucher arguments today. Many white liberals insist that decaying inner-city schools must be saved by forcing mostly African American children to stay put (no vouchers) but never dream of sending their own private- or suburban-school spawn to join them.

The sloping posture, the downward-folded hands as if in wrong-way prayer, the jowls, and the ski-jump nose joined forces to produce a cartoonist's dream come true: Richard M. Nixon. I hated the tricky one as much as the next college student, but I loved to draw him. There was something in his character that leached into his appearance. When he spoke in grave tones on television, even his body language seemed to be lying.

Nixon was a complex and polarizing figure long before I had any understanding of politics. My interest in him was simple. He was in charge of a war that could get me killed.

By the time I entered college in 1970, the student revolution had pretty much played out when four students at Kent State University were killed by their peers (many of whom were avoiding the draft) in the Ohio National Guard. There was little disagreement about the war in Vietnam. Everybody I knew was against it. Interest in politics was high, and it was personal. That's because any healthy eighteen-year-old boy without a student deferment was likely to be drafted. I entered college with such a deferment. Without it I might have been living abroad, either in Canada or Vietnam. Aside from recently graduated second lieutenants, the guys who couldn't afford higher education (or simply weren't college material) were the ones who got drafted. That injustice ended in 1971 when student deferments were replaced with a more suitable approach to senseless killing—a lottery.

Once everyone's butt was on the line, the Vietnam War wound down pretty quickly. The Nixon administration pressured South Vietnamese president Nguyen Van Thieu to accept a peace agreement with the North Vietnamese. The agreement called for Vietnamization, meaning that the United States could pull out of Vietnam and the South would take responsibility for its own defense. Nixon liked to call the agreement "peace with honor."

On the home front, Nixon was busy trying to preserve his own honor with a desperate coverup of a June 17, 1972, burglary of the Democratic election campaign headquarters in the Watergate building in Washington, D.C. The break-in was part of a larger effort to plant bugs, spy, generally mess things up for Democrats, and assure Nixon's reelection. He did get reelected in a landslide, but Watergate eventually assured his resignation.

The whole episode involved a series of events dating back to the publishing of the Pentagon Papers by the *New York Times* and *Washington Post* the week of

June 13, 1971. The Pentagon Papers were a top-secret analysis by the Defense Department of U.S. involvement in Vietnam. The report was leaked by Daniel Ellsberg, a Rand Corporation employee, who had become an antiwar activist. The Justice Department tried to block publication but was overruled by another landmark First Amendment decision by the Supreme Court on June 30. The court agreed with the *New York Times* that the government was using national security as an excuse to censor information about its policies.

Nixon evidently felt information about his policies did not belong on our breakfast tables. The White House established the so-called Plumbers group to plug inside leaks about the administration. One of the early break-ins by the Nixon burglary ring occurred when the Plumbers made a late-night house call to the office of Daniel Ellsberg's psychiatrist on September 3, 1971.

The Watergate saga was better reality television than Donald Trump's *Apprentice, Joe Millionaire,* and *Survivor* put together. Attorney General John Mitchell ran a slush fund for covert activities against the enemy, Democrats. Nixon's White House staff and the attorney general resigned over the scandal. White House Counsel John Dean was fired and later turned state's witness on Nixon before the Watergate Committee (with Hillary Clinton as counsel—we'll hear more about her later). On October 20, 1973, Nixon ordered Attorney General Elliot Richardson to fire Archibald Cox, the Justice Department's special prosecutor. Richardson refused and resigned. The order went down to Deputy Attorney General William Ruckelshaus, but he also refused and resigned. The dirty deed was finally carried out by Solicitor General Robert Bork (yes, we'll hear more about him too). This turn of events immediately became known as the Saturday Night Massacre.

On July 24, 1974, the Supreme Court ordered Nixon to turn over tapes he had secretly made of White House conversations. There was a mysterious eighteen-minute gap in a crucial conversation that secretary Rose Mary Woods testified she had accidentally erased. The House Judiciary Committee decided it had had enough and passed three articles of impeachment beginning July 27; Nixon resigned on August 8, 1974. Vice President Gerald Ford became president and pardoned Nixon on September 8, 1974.

Meanwhile, the Paris Peace Accord, negotiated by Henry Kissinger, had been signed on January 23, 1973. It cut American losses in Vietnam at 58,182 dead and ended U.S. military involvement in Vietnam. President Thieu felt the agreement sold out his country. On March 29, 1973, the last of the U.S. combat troops left Vietnam. In December 1974 the North Vietnamese broke the cease-fire agreement and attacked South Vietnamese forces. The United States protested but did not intervene, and by April 1975 Saigon was surrounded. President Ford refused military assistance. Thieu resigned on April 21, 1975, and Saigon fell nine days later.

In a letter to persuade Thieu to accept the accord, Nixon had written, "Should you decide, as I trust you will, to go with us, you have my assurance of continued assistance in the post settlement period and that we will respond with full force should the settlement be violated by North Vietnam. So once more I conclude with an appeal to you to close ranks with us." Apparently, he had his fingers crossed.

Thieu was publicly bitter about this. Nixon's exile in San Clemente, California, however, did not seem so bad, and I thought things might go swimmingly for President Thieu as well—especially since he was rumored to have checked through several tons of gold on his departure flight. If anyone had reason for hard feelings, it was the supporters he left behind.

Thieu's resignation struck me as an important event loaded with irony. Here he was leaving for a comfortable retirement, carping about being sold out, while the little guys stayed behind to take the bullets meant for him. In a sense, I suppose you could also say Thieu was the little guy left behind by Nixon. But the only bullets he'd be taking were silver ones—with an olive.

Big shots leaving messes for other people to clean up: it's a recurring theme when you draw presidents.

Gerald Ford was never forgiven for Nixon's pardon while he served out the remainder of the term. He also had to endure economic stagnation and inflation simultaneously. He suffered the pain of recession without the fun of low prices. Economists identified the peculiar condition by its scientific name, stagflation. Ford tried to control the inflation in part by peddling the infamous WIN buttons.

When Cambodia's Khmer Rouge captured the U.S. merchant ship *Mayaguez*, Ford responded forcefully by sending Marines to the wrong island, where they were cut down by entrenched Khmer forces. In a strange simultaneous happening, the *Mayaguez* was being peacefully released.

Ronald Reagan made a lively run at Ford in the Republican primary. Ford fought off that challenge, but bumbled through the general election, and in a debate with Jimmy Carter, prematurely proclaimed communist Poland a free country.

Perhaps the most gifted athlete ever to work in the Oval Office, Ford built a solid reputation as a klutz. He did physically stumble a few times, but his real clumsiness was at the helm, as he maneuvered the mighty ship of state through the treacherous shoals of stagflation, the Cold War, bad hair, leisure suits, and disco music that were the mid-seventies. He was, however, nimble enough to dodge Squeaky Fromme's potshot when the former Charles Manson acolyte tried to assassinate him.

His achievement of being named most valuable player of the 1934 University of Michigan football team wouldn't be repeated in the 1976 presidential campaign. He was a decent guy in an indecent time.

Decency became a new political ideal as the nation celebrated its bicentennial, and Jimmy Carter swept into office as the Anti-Nixon. He was a born-again Christian peanut farmer turned Southern politician. None of those things was anything I had experience with, and therefore, Mr. Carter was quite a novelty as he made his move to the national stage from the Georgia governor's mansion. He was bright, but so was Nixon. The thing that distinguished Carter was his combined claim to integrity and intelligence. The centerpiece of his campaign was his promise to never lie to the American people. Unlike Al Gore, he did not invent the Internet, but he was an engineer in the navy nuclear submarine program and he helped build the reactor for the first nuclear sub. He also had a great smile with a set of huge piano keys for teeth.

The nation was enthralled by Carter's eccentric family. "My mother went into the Peace Corps when she was sixty-eight. My one sister is a motorcycle freak, my other sister is a Holy Roller evangelist, and my brother is running for president. I'm the only sane one in the family," said Brother Billy, who appeared on the November 14, 1977, cover of *Newsweek* holding a can of his own brand, Billy Beer. He fit seamlessly into the tradition of huckster presidential brothers. In 1980 Billy was forced to register as a Libyan agent when it was learned he had received a $220,000 loan from the Libyan government. Predictably, a congressional investigation into "Billygate" followed.

Jimmy Carter was ahead of his time. Few consider that he was the first in presidential politics to issue a preemptive strike against possible future bimbo eruptions. He confessed in a *Playboy* interview that he had lusted in his heart for women other than his wife. Whether he ever disgraced the Oval Office with a lusting heart we'll probably never know. The *Playboy* interview wasn't quite the same as Bill Clinton's après–Super Bowl confession on *60 Minutes*. Nevertheless, it seemed enough to satisfy any strange concern voters might have harbored that their future commander-in-chief's heart-lusting days were behind him.

Unable to conceive of a future Bill Clinton, I considered Jimmy Carter to be obsessed by polls.

Carter inherited Federal Reserve chairman Arthur Burns from the Ford and Nixon administrations. Burns believed inflation was caused by a lack of discipline in government fiscal policy. He resigned in 1978, and Carter replaced him with Paul Volker, who finally strangled inflation during the Reagan administration with his tight money policy.

The beatific President Carter had an incredible lightness of being not shared by his close friend and adviser Bert Lance. The heavyset Lance was director of the Office of Management and Budget. He was forced to resign due to financial irregularities at Calhoun National Bank in Georgia, where he had been chairman before ascending, body and soul, to the right hand of power in the Carter administration.

"LONG LIVE THE FREE FRENCH OF QUEBEC"

Social upheaval wasn't limited to the United States. In Canada, the French separatist *Parti Québécois* came to power in Quebec in 1976, and in 1977 English-language schools were restricted and French was imposed as the province's language of business and government.

The highlight of the Carter administration was the Camp David Peace Accord signed by Israeli Prime Minister Menachim Begin and Egyptian President Anwar Sadat on September 17, 1978. Carter stayed holed up with Begin and Sadat for twelve days at the presidential retreat at Camp David, Maryland. After that they probably would have signed anything, but instead Israel agreed to return the Sinai Peninsula to Egypt in exchange for peace. Sadat was rewarded with a Nobel Prize, shared with Begin, in 1978 and with assassination in 1981.

On the other side of the ledger, President Carter withdrew support from the CIA-installed Shah of Iran, which allowed the Ayatollah Khomeini to rise to power in 1979. We got our first hint of where things were headed with Islamic fundamentalists when Carter let the shah into the United States for medical treatment on October 17, 1979. On November 4 the American Embassy in Tehran was overrun. The Iranians held fifty-two hostages in the embassy for 444 days, and Carter's inability to free them eventually cost him his job. The hostage crisis became a fog that wouldn't lift over the remainder of the Carter presidency. The president ordered a rescue attempt on April 24, 1980, that made President Ford's *Mayaguez* response look like a precision operation. Three of the eight helicopters involved failed in the sandy conditions, and the mission was cancelled. While evacuating the area, another chopper collided with a C-130 transport plane. Eight servicemen were killed; no hostages were rescued. An image of the disarray into which the U.S. military had fallen was beginning to emerge.

The Soviet Union invaded Afghanistan on December 24, 1979, and Carter's response was to boycott the 1980 Summer Olympics in Moscow. He lacked the courage or the vision to imagine a sequel to Jesse Owens's inspiring performance in the 1936 Berlin Olympics. The Winter Olympics were held in Lake Placid, New York. Jimmy Carter did not cancel, and the Soviets did not boycott. Fortunately, coach Herb Brooks and his team of overachieving American college boys had more than enough heart to make up for the wimp in the White House. They answered Jesse Owens's call by defeating the Soviet hockey team, one of the greatest teams ever, and winning the gold medal in the most inspiring miracle in U.S. sports history. We'll never know if that kind of latent greatness existed in any of our summer athletes. We knew for certain, however, that it did not dwell within the pure heart of Jimmy Carter.

Carter also took the heat for the lack of heat. The energy crisis dragged on and, although he could not create more fuel, Carter could, and did, create more government in the form of the new Department of Energy. Blame for the energy crisis couldn't fairly be pinned on Carter, but it was. Iran became an unreliable supplier of crude oil. More fundamentally, according to many economists, the wage price controls established by Richard Nixon had the effect of artificially depressing the supply of fuel. To his credit, Carter took steps to deregulate the fuel market, but since all bad things seemed to happen to Carter and all good things to Reagan, deregulation did not take effect until 1981, during the Reagan administration. All that voters got from Carter was a pep talk calling the energy crisis the moral equivalent of war and advice to wear sweaters and turn down their thermostats. The voters were not amused.

Note: Who says editors are worthless? I didn't have one when I drew this cartoon and misspelled "equivalent."

Sagging morale and soaring inflation drove the 1980 presidential campaign. The public was primed for Ronald Reagan's message of optimism and change. Carter seemed overwhelmed by the job, and what's more, people didn't like him. Reagan made no Poland gaffes in their debate on October 28, and people did like him. When Carter characterized Reagan as beginning his political career by campaigning against Medicare, Reagan famously responded, "There you go again." He went on to say that he simply had been in support of a competing piece of legislation to do the same job as Medicare but that he never opposed the principle of Medicare. Reagan was conservative but had long been portrayed in the national media as a right-wing extremist. When voters saw his good humor and winning way with people, they warmed to him and he defeated Carter in the November 4 election.

"DO YOU, MR.
EXECUTE

"...OF THE ABOVE, SOLEMNLY SWEAR TO FAITHFULLY ...FICE OF PRESIDENT OF THE UNITED STATES..."

In the 1980 presidential election, NBC projected Reagan the winner three hours before the polls closed on the West Coast. Many people didn't bother to vote after the network called the election, and they felt cheated.

Ronald Reagan, the 40th president of the United States, aliases:
Dutch, The Gipper.

CHAPTER 2

Ronald Reagan

President Reagan gave the appearance of a doddering old uncle, but in fact he was something of a fiery revolutionary.

His agenda was simple, and he stuck to it. He advanced the conservative fire Barry Goldwater had sparked as he went down in defeat to Lyndon Johnson in 1964. He was a different conservative from the establishment, country-club, minority-party version of the past. He had a more aggressive preference for individual self-reliance over government activism, which had been on the rise since Franklin Roosevelt. Reagan began his political life as an FDR Democrat but gradually came to believe that the role of the federal government had grown too large. He was also an ardent anticommunist. When he called the Soviet Union an evil empire, people believed he meant it. He had no problem with government, however, when he began a huge military buildup to oppose the Soviets.

His background as an actor served him well. He brought a new level of stage management to the presidency. He often went over the heads of Congress with direct television appeals to the public. He projected a sense of humor and humanity that carried him through rough patches like the Iran-Contra scandal that surely would have tripped up other presidents.

He pushed through a huge tax cut, which was followed by a brutal recession. He then raised taxes but called it "revenue enhancement," and no one complained. He presided over the downfall of the Soviet Union and a rebirth of American national self-esteem. People liked him. When Reagan died in 2004, Mikhail Gorbachev, leader of the "Evil Empire," eulogized his friend in the *New York Times*.

On January 20, 1981, Ronald Reagan was inaugurated as president of the

United States and, in a final snub to Jimmy Carter, the American hostages were released from Iran, 440 days after their capture. Reagan was elected on a platform of tax cuts, economic growth, limited government, and military expansion. Carter had tried to define him as a dangerous right-wing nut, but in a time of energy shortages, hopeless stagflation, and military decline, the voters saw only Reagan's sunny optimism.

In his acceptance speech at the Republican convention, Reagan said, "They say that the United States has had its day in the sun, that our nation has passed its zenith. They expect you to tell your children that the American people no longer have the will to cope with their problems, that the future will be one of sacrifice and few opportunities. My fellow citizens, I utterly reject that view." Apparently voters like that kind of talk. Reagan won forty-four states on election day.

His economic plan called for $41 billion in cuts in social programs, a 30 percent tax cut, increases in military spending, and no cuts to Social Security. The hope was that the tax cuts would stimulate enough economic growth to cover the lost revenue. Congress, not yet under Reagan's voodoo spell, proposed cuts in Social Security to cover the cost. Reagan rejected the bipartisan plan and then got shot by John Hinkley Jr. When he recovered, Congress was so glad to have him back it passed his economic plan.

Away from the supply side and on to the arms side, Reagan authorized the production of the neutron bomb as a deterrent to Soviet tank superiority against Western Europe. It may not have been exactly a smart bomb, but it wasn't stupid. Or nice. The idea was small blast, big radiation. The blast was too small to destroy tanks on the battlefield, but the radiation would melt the guys inside. Nearby cities would supposedly be spared. The tactical concern was that while radiation kills, it might do so too slowly, allowing the enemy to take offense and hit back before dying. Besides, a similar but cheaper weapon was already in production—cigarettes.

Smoking is really bad for you, but not quite as bad as the people who are always complaining about smoking.

Secretary of the Interior James Watt was a lightning rod for the Reagan administration on the environment, a tough job considering the Gipper himself once said that trees cause more pollution than automobiles.

Watt was a religious zealot, seemingly at odds with nature, who had a knack for driving environmentalists bonkers. When asked if we should preserve natural resources for future generations, he responded, "I don't know how many future generations we can count on before the Lord returns."

In 1983 he did what the Sierra Club never could do—he got himself fired when he paid his coal leasing commission this compliment: "We have every kind of mix you can have. I have a black, I have a woman, two Jews and a cripple, and we're good."

Reagan was spending like crazy trying to bankrupt the Russians before we bankrupted ourselves. He knew they would spend to keep up militarily. It was a good bet that they wouldn't try to match us on environmental spending, so why waste money on clean water?

These cartoons are from my environmentalist period. That period receded like the glaciers that once covered Ohio (without the benefit of man-made greenhouse gases, by the way). I am more skeptical now of the Greens since they've organized into an antiglobalism movement. I don't think they'll be satisfied until economic growth stops and we go back to a simpler, more pristine, self-sufficient time; a time when every house had a coal-burning furnace, and there was smoke in the sky and shit in the streets.

In the winter of 1988 an Ashland Oil company storage tank ruptured and spilled four million gallons of diesel oil into the Monongahela River. The oil then spilled out of Pennsylvania into the Ohio River. Drinking water for more than a million people was contaminated. (No word on whether they preferred it to regular Ohio River drinking water.)

CONSTRUCTIVE ENGAGEMENT

The apartheid government in South Africa offended the international community in 1985 and was subject to an economic boycott by the United Nations. Why, the southern United States had given up apartheid at least twenty years earlier. Aside from this embarrassing detail, South Africa was a thriving modern economy, and the Reagan administration saw no reason to ignore its more profitable virtues. A policy of constructive engagement was held to be a better way to modify the nasty behavior of the white South Africans. The theory was that the bad boys could be brought to heel more quickly through economic integration with the world than by isolation from it. In practice, the blacks did the constructing while the whites did the voting.

It is never acceptable to ridicule a country as backward if it lacks running water, proper sanitation, or considers collies central to the food pyramid. But if a country lacks, say, divorce on demand . . . go for it. Such was the case with Ireland when its people, in a California-style referendum, were so totally uncool as to choose to keep the practice of divorce illegal. This, of course, took place against a backdrop of a conflict in which it was entirely possible that an offending spouse would be blown to bits anyway because of his or her religion.

Where else can you find thoughtful analysis of complex issues like family planning, poverty, reproductive science, and Catholic Church doctrine all from one turnkey provider? Try your friendly local cartoonist.

Here's a slice of family life as television's alleged age of innocence collided with Dr. Everett Koop's war on AIDS. Maybe television was raunchy, even then, but parents weren't prepared to hear the surgeon general lecture their kids on the proper use of condoms. Little did they know they would soon learn about porn character Long Dong Silver in Judicial Committee hearings for the Supreme Court, not to mention blue dress stains in the Oval Office cigar room. Future concerns about condoms would merely be wardrobe decisions on HBO.

I'm not one of those lunatics who believe that all things good and bad flow from government action or inaction, and that therefore, because he was slow to act, Reagan caused the AIDS epidemic.

There's no doubt America was gripped by fear of HIV. It was an invisible and mysterious killer. Still, people needed to be scared out of their wits by something

BOK
©1987 AKRON BEACON JOURNAL

a little less abstract. They needed something that could strike anyone anywhere, like AIDS, but also something real with flashing, sharp teeth. Enter the pit bull. Once a few pit-bull attack stories appeared in the media, a wave of hysteria crashed over the country. If man managed to dodge the mystery virus, he still might be torn limb from limb by his best friend.

© 1987 AKRON BEACON JOURNAL

TV evangelist Jim Bakker, his wife, Tammy Faye, and her crying eyes hosted the PTL Club. He swindled his flock out of millions of dollars, pledged to build a Christian theme park called Heritage USA, and was sentenced to forty-five years in prison in 1989. He was paroled after serving five years. Things went south for the prosperous preacher in 1987 when it became clear he had oversold lifetime partnerships in Heritage USA. Details of his big spending included $265,000 to keep church secretary Jessica Hahn quiet about their affair. Bakker's crumbling empire was taken over by evangelist Jerry Falwell, while Hahn took the opportunity to leverage her cleavage into a *Playboy* spread.

Pat Robertson's Christian Coalition took political influence to the next level when he became a presidential candidate. Robertson carried a lot of baggage when it came to convincing the electorate. He had conspiracy theories about non-evangelical Christians, Jews, the Antichrist, and Methodists.

By 1986 Lady Liberty was looking shabby. After all those years standing in New York Harbor, America's gift from France was beginning to look like a prune. In celebration of her centennial, she was sent to Spa Iacocca to shape up. A committee to restore the Statue of Liberty was formed and funded by private donations and headed by Lee Iacocca, who had been spruced up himself with federal donations when his company, Chrysler, was bailed out by the Carter administration.

She was made quite beautiful again and was the debutante of a huge Fourth of July bash. The real belle of the ball, however, was Iacocca. It was supposed to be all about her, but it was all about him. The morning after she must have felt used. Nobody likes to see Lady Liberty not treated like a lady, and this cartoon drew a number of complaints. One caller was upset that the torch was in the wrong hand. Never mind that she was in bed.

Thank God she wasn't smoking.

"UMPH.. MY HEAD IS SPLITTING, LEE.. LEE?.. LEE?"

The mobile MX missile basing system was a scheme whereby nuclear missiles based in the United States would be loaded on railroad cars constantly in motion. The trick was that only some would be live missiles while the others would be dummies. That way the Soviets wouldn't know which ones to hit.

Ronald Reagan embarked on a space-based missile defense system. Its name was Strategic Defense Initiative (SDI), but everyone called it Star Wars. Star Wars would upset the existing defense system called Mutual Assured Destruction (MAD). Mutual Assured Destruction meant what it said: shoot off a nuke and we all die, so don't do it. Important establishment thinkers supported MAD and said Star Wars was insane. MAD did preserve a balance between the nuclear superpowers that made a first strike unthinkable. It also preserved the Cold War status quo, and now a conservative president was promoting change in a big way. He even offered to share it with the Soviets.

At a historic summit in Reykjavik, Iceland, on October 11, 1986, General Secretary Mikhail S. Gorbachev and Reagan shared their desire to eliminate nuclear weapons. Gorby tried to get an agreement on European short-range nuclear missiles but yanked the ball away on Star Wars. Both leaders came away with nothing but a better understanding of each other.

Lucy pulling the ball away as Charlie Brown is about to kick it is an image endowed to cartoondom by the late great Charles Schulz (hereafter referred to as Sparky). This cartoon may not be the cutting edge of originality, but I wanted to do it anyway because Reagan was, after all, the Gipper.

Reagan and Gorbachev signed the INF treaty in 1987 to eliminate intermediate-range nuclear missiles. The treaty required each side to be monitored by the other through regular inspections. Reagan called it "trust but verify." He and Gorbachev were friendly, and Gorby was a big hit with the American public. He was a prophet with somewhat less honor in his own land. The Soviet economy was in the tank. The INF agreement was something he had to accept because of growing Soviet weakness and inability to respond to the Pershing short-range nukes Reagan had deployed in Europe. The Gipper had his own cold warriors to deal with at home, and they were not interested in trusting or verifying.

In an effort to block communist expansion in Central America, President Reagan sought to isolate the Sandinista government in Nicaragua, led by Daniel Ortega. Reagan claimed the Sandinistas were supplying guerrillas in El Salvador with weapons from Cuba. Nicaragua denied the charge. Nevertheless, on January 23, 1981, the United States suspended all aid to Nicaragua. The United States also began supporting groups in Honduras known as the Contras, made up of Anastasio Somoza's former national guard members. The Contras along with other guerrillas, including popular former Sandinista Eden Pastora, began to do serious damage to the Nicaraguan economy with hit-and-run attacks.

As a result, the Sandinistas cracked down and outlawed political opposition. Money was diverted to the military, and agriculture failed.

Four young men accosted Bernard Goetz in a subway car in Manhattan on December 22, 1984. They wanted $5. They got lead. Goetz, a two-time subway mugging victim, whipped out his peace maker and commenced firing. Goetz was acquitted of attempted murder and assault charges but convicted of unlicensed possession of a deadly weapon, and served 250 days in jail. To many Americans fed up with crime, he became a hero known as the Subway Vigilante. To others he was a symbol of racism, oppression, and the general unwillingness of the ruling class to share its wealth with less fortunate muggers.

Ronald Reagan could be viewed in the same way. In his world, Daniel Ortega and the Sandinistas were the thugs who took over subway Nicaragua. Reagan used unauthorized firepower, in an extralegal action, and came out guns blazing. People complained, but many were quietly pleased to see the punks plugged.

Reagan had better counsel than Goetz. He came out with no attempted murder or assault charges and beat the weapons rap in the Iran-Contra Senate hearings. Vigilante international.

THE VIGILANTE

Admiral John Poindexter served as Reagan's national security adviser in 1986. He was in charge of the scheme to divert money from the secret sale of arms to Iran to the Contras in Nicaragua. The Contras were a U.S. administration-backed guerrilla force trying to overthrow the Sandinista government. The U.S. Congress had denied them funds. It wasn't pretty. Poindexter was given immunity to testify before Congress about the affair. He said, "I made a very deliberate decision not to tell the president so that I could insulate him from the decision and provide some future deniability for the president if it ever leaked out." Great—the president is ignorant of his own policy. Reagan was severely damaged under Poindexter's protection but survived.

Poindexter resurfaced in the Bush II administration as head of the Information Assurance Office at the Department of Defense Advanced Research Projects Agency. He was fired after dreaming up a plan to create a market in terrorism futures.

"GO AHEAD AND EAT IT. OLLIE NORTH SAYS THAT IT WILL GIVE US PLAUSIBLE DENIABILITY."

While Poindexter was the brains of the operation, Oliver North was running Iran-Contra from the White House basement. Ollie and his secretary, the fetching Fawn Hall, shredded documents there, under the president's nose, to give him plausible deniability. In the Iran-Contra universe, plausible deniability was paradise, the most desired state of mindless bliss.

In its 1987 ruling in *U.S. v. Salerno* the Supreme Court said that pretrial detention based on "dangerousness" is a legitimate regulatory function—not punishment. In other words, you can be jailed before you are convicted and not just to make sure you show up. Meanwhile, a convicted rapist was released early from a California prison and promptly raped a young woman and cut off her arms.

"I'M SORRY, SIR, BUT IF WE DON'T GET CONGRESSIONONAL APPROVAL WE CAN'T JUST APPOINT A SUPREME COURT JUSTICE ANYWAY AND NOT TELL ANYONE."

Since Robert Bork's failed 1987 Supreme Court nomination, we've had a politics of recrimination that seems to get more bitter with each election cycle. The Democrats rejected Bork, the Republicans nominated Clarence Thomas, and the Dems dug up Anita Hill. Thomas played the race card and won.

Democrats tricked Bush into breaking his no-tax pledge, causing Bill Clinton to win. Clinton's wife immediately began telling everybody what was good for them, culminating with her health plan. Republicans killed the plan, stiffed Clinton's court nominations, and impeached him. Clinton tried to pass the torch to the insufferable Al Gore, who won the popular vote but lost the electoral vote to hanging chads and demented voters in Broward County, Florida. Gore challenged the 2000 election, brought in Jesse Jackson to play the race card with a vengeance, and lost. As with all big issues these days, the election was forced into the U.S. Supreme Court, and there the court majority, including Justice Thomas, awarded the election to George W. Bush.

That left us with a Democratic Party nursing an obsessive hatred of Bush. Meanwhile Bush's "conservative" court upheld racial quotas, found a constitutional right to sodomy, and moved toward performing gay marriages in its spare time. This may not be good for the country but it's good for the cartoon business.

After the Big Borking, Reagan nominated Douglas Ginsburg for the Supreme Court in 1987. The House Judiciary Committee tried to pin him down on a conflict of interest with cable television stock he owned. The point became moot when he admitted smoking dope with his Harvard students. Wonder if any of them will make it to the high court.

"Well, shouldn't you step aside, Mr. Attorney General?"

"Don't you think that it hurts him [Reagan] to have you there? Don't you think that maybe for his sake you might step aside?"

"If you are indicted, will you step aside?"

—Sam Donaldson's questions to Ed Meese,
This Week with David Brinkley, March 13, 1988

"If honest public officials can be hounded out of office by partisan political attacks and media barrages, then no public official is safe."

—Meese response

"Meese could still face a Justice Department investigation for non-criminal ethics violations. But meanwhile, since he was not indicted, he is now entitled to ask the taxpayers to pick up his legal bill for more than $250,000."

—Reporter Rita Braver, *CBS Evening News*, July 18, 1988

In his 1988 book, *Speaking Out*, press secretary Larry Speakes claimed he made up quotes about facts and details and attributed them to big picture guy President Reagan in press briefings.

Speaking of made-up quotes, after John Hinkley's March 1981 assassination attempt on the president, Nancy Reagan began consulting on a regular basis with astrologer Joan Quigley. Nancy would give the president's schedule to the prognosticator, whose job was to align it with the appropriate stars, planets, and black holes. Nancy would then insist that the White House staff make the appropriate schedule adjustments, and Nancy was obeyed. I suppose it couldn't hurt to know that the man with his finger on the button had all his stars in a row.

As chairman of the Federal Reserve Board, Paul Volker put the squeeze on the nation's money supply, bringing the inflation rate down from 14.8 percent to 4 percent in three years, beginning in 1980. That killed the economic stagflation that snuffed Jimmy Carter's presidency. The cigar-smoking Volker also had more success than President Ford's strategy of issuing "Whip Inflation Now" WIN buttons. When Reagan appointed Alan Greenspan Fed chairman in 1987, it seemed unlikely anyone could fill Volker's Florsheims. As it turned out, Greenspan whipped inflation now until some big thinkers actually began to worry about deflation following the 2002 economic downturn. His highest accolade came with John McCain's 2000 campaign promise that if Greenspan died he would "prop him up and put sunglasses on him like they did in the movie *Weekend at Bernie's*".

Bush sought the Republican nomination for the 1988 presidential election and found it difficult to gain attention and traction while serving as vice president to the spotlight-savvy Reagan.

George Herbert Walker Bush had run against Reagan for the 1980 Republican nomination. Reagan's platform was for increased military spending and tax cuts. Reagan subscribed to a theory called "supply-side economics," illustrated by the Laffer Curve, cooked up by economist Arthur Laffer. He predicted the tax cuts would cause so much new economic activity that tax revenues would increase enough to replace the money lost through tax cuts. During the campaign Bush called it voodoo economics. When the vanquished primary candidate Bush later became Reagan's vp, many true believers questioned his conversion.

Nancy Reagan brought a new sense of high style to the White House. Johnny Carson joked that her favorite junk food was caviar. By the time the Reagans left office in 1989 she had worn more than three hundred designer dresses worth an estimated total of $1.4 million. They were "borrowed" and therefore not taxed as income. They must have been supply-side dresses.

The so-called wimp factor dogged Bush as he followed the robust Reagan presidency. Fortune smiled on him when he drew his Democratic opponent, Governor Michael Dukakis of Massachusetts, who was perceived as weak on defense. Meanwhile Reagan and Gorbachev played kissy face over the INF treaty and set about disarming the nuclear threat.

The wimp factor was really a creation of the press.

George Bush made Michael Dukakis's patriotism a campaign issue when Dukakis said he would not require Massachusetts schoolchildren to recite the Pledge of Allegiance. Bush visited flag factories, was photographed in front of flags, and made it a point to be especially opposed to burning the American flag.

Mike Dukakis's running mate was Lloyd Bentsen, a U.S. senator from Texas. As chairman of the Senate Finance Committee, Bentsen had a fundraising gimmick called the "Chairman's Club." It was a $10,000 cash-for-access proposition that earned the contributor breakfast with Lloyd once a month. When the brunch bunch story hit page 1 of the *Washington Post*, Bentsen apologized and gave back all the money. Such a bald-faced $10,000 pay-to-play scheme is shocking. That sort of access is easily worth $100,000 today.

Bush's running mate, Dan Quayle, was a wealthy forty-one-year-old blow-dried senator from Indiana. He didn't have much high-level experience beyond his golf game and provided quite a contrast to the smooth, silver-haired and -tongued Bentsen.

He shared a trait common to many presidential politicians. They consciously or subconsciously affected the mannerisms and appearance, especially the hairdo, of President John F. Kennedy.

During the 1988 vice presidential debate in Omaha, Quayle attempted to defend his youth and inexperience by claiming a Senate tenure similar to that of John F. Kennedy. Lloyd Bentsen seemed to anticipate this and called him on it, saying, "Senator, I served with Jack Kennedy. I knew Jack Kennedy. Jack Kennedy was a friend of mine. Senator, you're no Jack Kennedy." It was a great put down and it stuck.

The thing is, Dukakis had the Kennedy hand motions down cold, plus he was from Massachusetts and had an LBJ-slick running mate from Texas.

Bush struggled with the dual duties of running for president and serving as vice president to a man with real charm.

BERNHARD GOETZ

SUBWAY VIGILANTE

CARL ROWAN

SUBURB VIGILANTE

Maybe this one should say syndicated vigilante. Syndicated columnist Carl Rowan was a scourge of handgun owners. In 1981 he wrote, "We must reverse this psychology [of needing guns for home defense]. We can do it by passing a law that says anyone found in possession of a handgun, except a legitimate officer of the law, goes to jail—period!"

In the middle of an August night in 1988, he was startled by an unexpected pool party in his backyard. As the intruders were leaving, Rowan did what any enlightened liberal writer would do. He shot one of them with his unregistered handgun.

Evidence of a program of secret weapons of mass destruction was found outside Cincinnati, Ohio, at the Fernald Feed Materials Production Center. The 1,050-acre site processed uranium for use in the U.S. atomic weapons program from 1951 to 1988. Radioactive material from the plant contaminated ground and surface water, including the aquifer feeding the great Miami River.

In *Cipollone v. Liggett & Meyers Group Inc.* a jury, in 1988, made the first-ever award in a tobacco liability case. Tobacco companies felt they had ironclad protection due to the warnings on packs of cigarettes.

I drew this cartoon before I had encountered my 1,000th homeless panhandler.

"IMPROPER?... WHY NO, I HAVEN'T NOTICED ANYTHING IMPROPER."

Something about that Iraqi oil pipeline. This was drawn in 1988 with Ed Meese as the beneficiary. In December 2003, I saw a cartoon of the Iraqi pipeline going through Dick Cheney's Haliburton Corp. head.

On July 3, 1988 (when Iraq was our ally), the USS *Vincennes*, a cruiser under the command of Captain Will Rogers III in the Persian Gulf, engaged lightly armed Iranian gunboats that were harassing shipping in the Strait of Hormuz. The *Vincennes* was a billion-dollar ship designed for complex combat with the Soviet navy and equipped with the U.S. Navy's most sophisticated Aegis radar and battle equipment. It fired on the speedboats with five-inch guns, sinking two. During the skirmish the Aegis system detected what it thought was an attacking Iranian F14 fighter jet. The *Vincennes* fired Standard surface-to-air missiles and knocked an Iranian Airlines wide-bodied Airbus A300 out of the sky, creating 290 dead civilians.

The Worker Adjustment and Retraining Notification Act (WARN) was signed into law by President Reagan on August 4, 1988. It required companies of one hundred or more full-time employees to give sixty days' notice in advance of major layoffs. Reagan resisted the legislation. One argument against it was that workers on sixty days' notice would lack the incentive to produce quality work and might even sabotage their company. Ronald Reagan's second term ended within sixty days of the law's enactment.

George Herbert Walker Bush, 41st president of the United States, alias: Poppy.

CHAPTER 3

George Herbert Walker Bush

Geeorge H. W. began jumping out of airplanes as a naval aviator in the Pacific in World War II when his plane was hit by enemy fire. He survived, but two crewmen did not. He resumed his jumping career to celebrate his seventy-fifth birthday and then again on his eightieth. Both times he chose to jump out of "perfectly good airplanes," as his wife Barbara put it. Maybe he was trying to ditch his Secret Service guys.

Poppy, like Gerald Ford, was a legitimate college athlete. He was a first baseman and captain of the Yale baseball team.

He was the son of a wealthy eastern establishment family who moved to Texas to establish himself in the oil business. He later followed in the family tradition of public service.

As president he enjoyed a 90 percent approval rating after defeating Iraq, yet he suffered political defeat himself after serving one term.

George Herbert Walker Bush was able to slip the Reagan shadow long enough to kill off the Mike Dukakis challenge to his inheritance of the Reagan presidency. Bush was helped by an ad that hammered Dukakis for the Massachusetts prison furlough program. Willie Horton, a convicted murderer, had been released from prison on a weekend pass. While out, he assaulted a man and raped his wife. Bush painted Dukakis as a soft-on-crime Brookline, Taxachusetts liberal. Dukakis didn't help himself when in the second presidential debate, Bernard Shaw, of CNN, asked him if he would support the death penalty for someone who raped and murdered his wife. Dukakis didn't say, "Hell, yes" or "Who do you think you are to ask me such a rude and impertinent question?" Instead, he answered like a lawyer and pretty much killed what small hope he had of becoming president. He extinguished any remaining spark of life in his presidential bid by posing for a ridiculous photo in a tank wearing an unflattering helmet.

Bush's legacy from Reagan was a lingering budget deficit to go along with his own campaign pledge of "Read my lips, no new taxes." At the same time, globalism was becoming an overwhelming force, and Japan, with its protected industries, seemed to be eating our lunch in world trade. Everything they made seemed better and cheaper, and Americans had the nerve to buy it. The U.S. trade deficit with Japan in 1989 was $51.7 billion. The Super 301 provisions of the Omnibus Trade and Competitiveness Act of 1988 were an effort to open Japan to U.S. competition. Meaning we would force them to buy our stuff. A desperate nation begged its cartoonists for wisdom on trade policy.

The "Buy America" issue wasn't as simple as it seemed.

"WHOSE BRIGHT IDEA WAS IT TO CUT BACK THE OIL SPILL CLEAN-UP DEPARTMENT ANYWAY?"

In 1988 thousands of fish and birds, including 150 bald eagles, perished in the most expensive DUI case ever, when the Exxon *Valdez* oil tanker cracked in Prince William Sound, Alaska. The helmsman and third mate were at the wheel while captain Joe Hazelwood slept off a bender. The ship ran aground, spilling eleven million gallons of crude over 1,300 miles of coastline.

It cost $7 billion to clean up the mess, including fines and damages. The Exxon company brought the cleanup to a halt in September 1989.

THE BUCK STOPS HERE

In addition to the Sandinista regime in Nicaragua, the United States also resisted the Farabundo Marti National Liberation Front (FMLN) in El Salvador. The purpose was to prevent communist expansion in this hemisphere. This meant propping up an especially brutal civilian/military junta in El Salvador. The war left 75,000 dead. It was bookended by the murder of Archbishop Oscar Romero in San Salvador as he celebrated Mass on March 24, 1980 and the torture murders of six Jesuits at the University of San Salvador in 1989.

In making the pitch to the American public for aid to the Contras to fight the Sandinistas in Nicaragua, President Reagan wanted to convince Americans that a threat, if not imminent, was at least near. So he insisted that the Nicaraguan Red Menace was a mere two days' drive from Harlingen, Texas. With the defeat of Ortega and the Sandinistas in 1990, we could only imagine the relief of the good people of Harlingen.

The Sandinistas and the FMLN fell in Central America while the Soviet Union was disintegrating in Europe and Asia. Only the bearded one from Cuba remained in the dictators' sun room.

"*The truth is not simply what you think it is; it is also the circumstances in which it is said, and to whom, why and how it is said.*" Vaclav Havel, a playwright, wrote those words and served almost five years in prison in his native Czechoslovakia. He believed moral resistance and the truth were the keys to survival in a Czechoslovakian totalitarian system that crushed the will and dignity of its people. On December 22, 1989, by a unanimous vote of the Federal Assembly, he was elected president of a newly free Czechoslovakia, and on February 21, 1990, he addressed a joint session of the U.S. Congress. Times change.

Ronald Reagan, a former actor, was steadfast in his opposition to communism and played a role in the freedom that came to Soviet bloc countries including Czechoslovakia. One of Reagan's anticommunist causes was funding of the Contra opposition in Nicaragua. Congress had refused funding for the Contras, so the money came from illegal arms sales to Iran, directed from Ollie North and John Poindexter's shop in the White House basement. During seven hours of videotaped testimony in John Poindexter's Iran-Contra trial the president denied knowing anything about it. Maybe he didn't. Or maybe he just had a different approach than Vaclav Havel.

Glasnost is a Russian term related to the word voice—meaning openness or transparency. Gorbachev introduced a new openness in Soviet society that literally gave voice to the people. He freed the dissident Andrei Sakharov from internal exile and gave an honest accounting of the country's current economic meltdown. The population raised its new voice by electing Gorbachev's opponent, Boris Yeltsin, to the legislature. The Communist Party lost its grip on power and the republics began moving for independence.

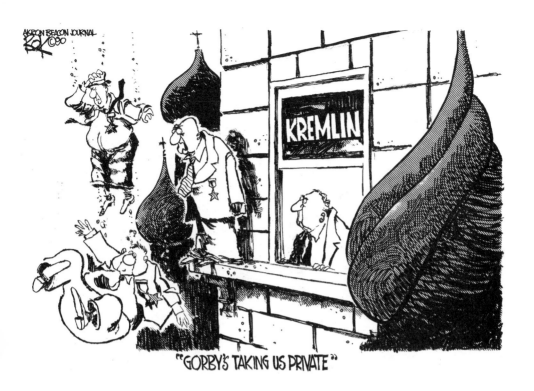

"GORBY'S TAKING US PRIVATE"

Glasnost and *perestroika* were an effort to roll back the effects of Stalinism and save the Soviet Union from economic collapse. It must have seemed overwhelming to party officials. After the sixty-year economic bubble of central planning, they were used to full employment and job security, except for the occasional purge.

"WELL, MIKHAIL, WE DID WHAT THEY SAID COULD NEVER BE DONE... WE PUT THE GENIE BACK IN THE BOTTLE."

Bush and Gorbachev signed the Joint Statement on the Treaty on Strategic Offensive Arms at a Washington summit in June 1990. They signed the actual START I treaty the following July. The START agreement was the first to actually reduce nuclear weapons. Just as the superpowers were agreeing to eliminate the nuclear stockpile, Iraq was invading Kuwait. The focus of weapons of mass destruction fears shifted from the Evil Empire to the Axis of Evil.

THE MOTHER OF ALL WARS

When Bush said Iraq's invasion of Kuwait would not stand, he backed it up with an impressive military victory with international support. Americans seemed to come out of their Vietnam War funk. The military was once again respected and there were causes worth fighting for, like oil. The nation was proud of its Gulf War veterans, but the same still couldn't be said for their hard-luck Vietnam War brethren. The only euphoria associated with them was drug-related.

Pete Rose denied betting on baseball but not selling autographs.

Commissioner Bart Giamatti banned him from baseball for life on August 24, 1989, for betting on the game. Giamatti died of a heart attack September 1, 1989. Pete went to prison on August 10, 1990, on an income tax rap related to gambling income.

The United States was working on a cocaine habit in the 1980s. Two Colombian organizations, the Medellin and Cali cartels, competed vigorously to satisfy that habit. Three Colombian presidential candidates were assassinated in 1989 and 1990. President Bush attended a summit on illicit drug trafficking in Cartagena, Colombia, February 15, 1990, and it created quite a stir with regard to the president's safety. Considering the crime rate in Washington, D.C., President Bush did the wise thing by hightailing it to the relative safety of Pablo Escobar's Colombia.

A stealthy and skittish House of Representatives passed itself a 25 percent pay hike plus cost of living raises in the middle of the night on November 17, 1989. The less brazen Senate was punished for its lack of support with a mere 10 percent increase. In a remarkable display of bipartisanship, House leaders on both sides promised to defend members of the opposing party from political attack for supporting the pay hike. Hardly a word of protest was heard—just skittery little scratchy sounds.

Budget Director Richard Darman fretted quite a bit about balancing the budget—especially in light of President Bush's understated campaign pledge: "Read my lips, no new taxes." Eventually Darman convinced Bush to raise taxes, sealing his fate, if not his lips, as a one-term president.

The IRS may not be able to give you the right answer about its own tax rules, but it does manage to find you. The U.S. Census, on the other hand, estimates it missed eight million people in 1990.

The Savings and Loan scandal eventually cost American taxpayers $157 billion to bail out the insolvent institutions through the Federal Savings and Loan Deposit Insurance Corporation. President Bush's son Neil's name turned up during the investigation of an unsavory S&L. This must have worried his father, who chose only nonfinancial felons as friends.

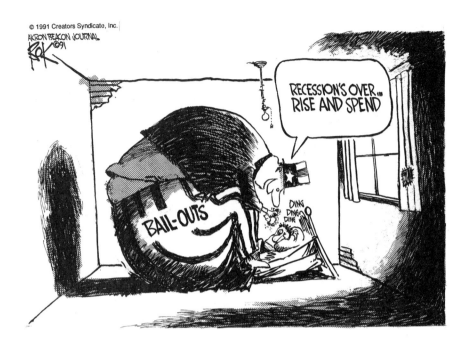

Having done its part in bailing out the S&L industry, the feds called on consumers to do their part and spend like mad into prosperity.

Politicians love family values. Simon & Shuster published Kitty Kelley's *Nancy Reagan: The Unauthorized Biography* in 1991. It was filled with gossip about a dysfunctional Reagan family, including Nancy's astrology, her "long lunches" with Frank Sinatra, and the Gipper's alleged lack of interest in his children. Personally, I find a refusal to spend a lifetime hustling kids to practices, camps, and clinics refreshingly healthy.

Meanwhile Ted Kennedy bonded with his son Patrick and nephew William Kennedy Smith for a night of wilding in Palm Beach. William Kennedy Smith was acquitted of rape charges, stemming from the boys' night out, in a West Palm Beach media circus tent, er, courtroom on December 11, 1991.

Salvador Dali, 1904–1989.

Theodore Geisel, aka Dr. Seuss, dead I am. March 2, 1904–September 24, 1991.

The Centers for Disease Control recommended that doctors and dentists should test themselves for AIDS, as the epidemic spread in 1991. In a Gallup Poll commissioned by *Newsweek*, 94 percent of Americans agreed. Ben Schatz, attorney for the American Association of Physicians for Human Rights, feared a witch hunt against infected health care workers. Mr. Schatz may have been on to something. Senator Jesse Helms proposed legislation calling for a ten-year prison sentence and $10,000 fine for any HIV-infected health care worker who failed to disclose his or her condition to a patient.

Having reckoned with the school crisis and the S&L crisis, a grateful nation turned its gaze to Uncle Sam, in the spring of 1991, to solve the health care crisis.

The Clintons and Gores showed up in Sin City (New York) for the 1992 Democratic convention.

Billionaire populist Ross Perot drew 20 percent of the popular vote in the 1992 election. He didn't formally declare his candidacy until summer. Bush and Clinton both groveled at the feet of the sixty-million-dollar-campaign man. Some would quibble with the term "grovel" and simply call it acting presidential.

Bill Clinton, 42nd president of the United States, aliases: Bubba, Slick Willie.

CHAPTER 4

William Jefferson Clinton

Bill Clinton, the first baby boomer president, was a man of undiscriminating appetites and unmet potential. He grew up in difficult circumstances in Arkansas and went on to become a Rhodes Scholar and, later, the master politician of his age. He saved the Democratic Party from oblivion by recognizing the shift Ronald Reagan had caused in American politics. He moved his party to the center and from there was able to govern as a two-term president.

He stumbled out of the blocks with his campaign pledge to allow gays in the military. Then he put his wife in charge of a task force to reform health care. The task force was secretive, and when the breadth of its proposal to manage 13 percent of the U.S. economy became apparent, Congress rejected it.

Clinton was dogged by questions about a real estate investment scheme, known as Whitewater, while he was governor of Arkansas in the 1980s. The Whitewater scandal evolved into a sex scandal when his affair with White House intern Monica Lewinsky spilled onto the front pages. He was impeached but remained in office to finish his term.

President Clinton was a larger-than-life figure for whom cartoonists are very grateful.

George Bush's 90 percent approval rating following Desert Storm didn't provide him enough political capital to cover him when he broke his pledge of no new taxes. Clinton was relentless in overcoming early whiffs of scandal and so-called bimbo eruptions in the 1992 campaign. His motto was "It's the economy, stupid." He insisted that Bush presided over the worst economy in forty years. There was as much truth to that statement as there was to his later claim, "I never had sex with that woman." The 1991–92 economic downturn was only a temporary blip, but

Clinton stayed on message and, with the help of Ross Perot's vote-splitting candidacy, he slid into the White House.

When the Clintons moved into their new home at 1600 Pennsylvania Avenue, they were faced with the same problem as all itinerant parents. Where would they send their kid to school? Previous occupants of the house, the plain-folk Carters, also had a daughter, and they chose to send her to the local public school. They did this because they wanted the neighbors to know they were plain folks but also because they were cheap.

The Clintons were very vocal about their support for the public schools too, as the teachers' union had been vocal about its support for the Clintons. They opposed vouchers that would be paid for with public money to allow children a choice other than the local Washington, D.C., public schools which, as it happened, were the worst in the nation. The Clinton family's choice was to send their daughter to the very expensive and very private Sidwell Friends School because they were not cheap. The underprivileged, as always, would go it alone in the worst schools in the country. The Clinton family supported the public schools with their words, and in the Clinton family, saying it is enough.

The first indication that things would be different under the Clinton administration was when old-fashioned taxing and spending became taxing and "investing."

As a result of Bill Clinton's campaign promise to lift the ban on gays in the military, two sailors who weren't asked decided to tell anyway. They came out of the closet in 1992 and proclaimed their homosexuality on national television. The subsequent military and civilian backlash resulted in the compromise Don't Ask, Don't Tell policy.

Five thousand people attended Tailhook '91 in Las Vegas, a three-day convention of navy and marine aviators, defense contractors, and civilian employees. In addition to military stuff, the agenda included leg shaving; mooning against window panes (a pane was pushed out and crashed into the pool area due to excess bare buttock p.s.i.); wearing rhino horns and drinking "rhino spunk" from a strategically located rhino dildo; the gauntlet, consisting of two or three hundred men lining a hallway to grope women as they passed through; ball walking, which is strolling with one's testicles hanging out, a popular activity; butt biting; and strippers. A good time was had by all except the eighty-seven women and three men who were assaulted. After a lengthy investigation and much publicity, 140 navy and marine officers were referred for disciplinary action. Secretary of the Navy H. Lawrence Garrett III resigned.

Sexual harassment issues moved from the workplace to the classroom in 1993, when the American Association of University Women issued a report called *Hostile Hallways*, the first national study of sexual harassment in public schools.

By 1993 the government and the media had us looking for perverts at work, at day care, in our homes, and under our own beds. The hyperactive Janet Reno played a large role in this because of her Concern for Children.

Before broiling a number of children in the Branch Davidian compound as attorney general of the United States, Reno was ringleader of a show trial in Dade County, Florida, where she was district attorney.

Frank Fuster was convicted of molesting children at the Country Walk day care service he operated with his wife, Ileana. He was convicted, without physical evidence, based on testimony coerced from small children by a couple of self-styled court psychologists, Lauri and Joseph Braga. The Bragas used "anatomically correct dolls" and proposed weird tales of nasty treatment of their naughty bits by the Fusters. Eventually the kids caved, no doubt to get rid of the real child abusers, the Bragas, and ratted out Frank Fuster to prison. Reno's innovative courtroom technique touched off a national wave of child abuse hysteria that resulted in similar legal outrages in Massachusetts, Washington State, and California.

ANOTHER REASON THEY CAN'T READ

Bob Packwood resigned from the U.S. Senate after the Senate Ethics Committee unanimously recommended he do so for his "offensive and degrading sexual misconduct." He was found to have sexually harassed at least seventeen women. His personal diary was subpoenaed and revealed he'd had sex with twenty-two senate staffers. It was the behavior of a goatlike older guy with bad hair, clutching, grabbing, and getting into tongue twisters you don't want to think about. There were, however, no accusations (as far as I know) of uninvited displays of his packwoody.

The National Organization for Women was the driving force in his downfall.

Where was NOW during the Clinton wildwoody days?

In a letter that surfaced during congressional hearings in 1994, Ann Lewis, assigned by the Resolution Trust Corporation to investigate Whitewater, wrote that Clinton "was a lying bastard."

On April 19, 1993, I watched a foreshadowing of September 11, 2001, on television. The FBI decided to end the fifty-one-day siege of the Branch Davidian compound in Waco, Texas. David Koresh and about eighty followers, including women and children, had been holed up there since Alcohol, Tobacco and Firearms agents tried to arrest Koresh on a minor charge and seize weapons, touching off a gun battle that left ten dead, including four ATF agents. The FBI used pyrotechnic tear gas grenades, which touched off a blaze that killed everyone inside. All on live television. It was a disturbing sight. This wasn't an attack by suicidal religious fanatics. It was the government killing religious fanatics.

Attorney General Janet Reno took the arrows of full responsibility for Bill Clinton. The FBI apparently was paying attention to the threat from religious fundamentalists. Just the wrong ones.

IN THE AFTERMATH OF THE WACO TRAGEDY BILL FINDS THE WOMAN OF HIS DREAMS

Trickle down was more than an economic theory to the Reagan administration. Saying No to Drugs wasn't enough. You must say yes to peeing into a cup if you worked for the government after The Gipper signed the Civilian Testing Program executive order in 1986. Unless you were Secretary of State George Schultz, who said no way. As the war on drugs escalated, testing became common in the private sector also. The Clinton administration was famous for its war on drug companies. Antipathy toward drug makers didn't inhibit Clinton's well-known propensity for soliciting campaign contributions. Clinton-Gore obtained $250,000 in gifts or loans from pharmaceutical firms for the 1993 inauguration. They landed $582,945 in hard and soft drug money contributions for the 1992 and 1996 campaigns.

"O.K., BORIS, NOW THAT YOU'VE MASTERED THE VETO, LET'S MOVE ON TO THE MORE SUBTLE ASPECTS OF DEMOCRACY."

In 1993 Boris Yeltsin, the tipsy populist Russian president, illegally suspended the duma, or parliament, when it refused to cooperate with his privatization plan for the Russian economy. Parliament resisted and took up arms. Yeltsin took control of the military and blasted a hole in the parliament building, bringing fresh air and new light to Russian politics.

North Korea is an isolated country. There is nothing more annoying to an isolationist than overly empathetic people. This is why Bill Clinton was the perfect guy to negotiate a new inspections agreement when Kim Ill Jung violated the old one. North Korea refused to permit the International Atomic Energy Agency to inspect two undeclared nuclear sites on February 10, 1993. The North threatened to withdraw from the Nuclear Non-Proliferation Treaty, and the possibility of war became a concern. Clinton became heavily involved, and on October 21, 1994, the Agreed Framework was signed.

As Bush was leaving office, American, British, and French fighters offered Saddam a parting shot by bombing sites in Iraq on January 13, 1993. On April 14, 1993, Kuwaiti security broke up an Iraqi attempt to assassinate the former president Bush with a car bomb while he visited Kuwait. Saddam had miscalculated again. Presidents evidently stick together on these things, because on June 26 Bill Clinton unloaded twenty-three Tomahawk guided missiles on Iraq.

LEGACY

One president and four ex-presidents showed up in Yorba Linda, California, for Richard M. Nixon's funeral on April 27, 1994. Nixon was a polarizing figure, which means everybody hated him. But they were all there for his funeral and they all had something nice to say about him. As they gave their eulogies, I wondered what they were really thinking. Then it hit me. If it weren't for Nixon none of them would be president.

Bob Hope got former presidents Ford and Bush together, along with President Clinton, for the 1995 Bob Hope Chrysler Classic golf tournament. Once again, President Ford got the short end of the stick (note the helmets on the spectators and the lump on his head).

Nicole Brown Simpson and Ronald Goldman were hacked to death on June 12, 1994. On June 17, O.J. Simpson made his own personal freedom ride in a white Ford Bronco. From that point forward, the high-priced legal dream team of F. Lee Bailey, Johnny Cochran, and Marvin Shapiro laid siege to the legal system for sixteen months, portraying O.J. as an exploited racial victim of the white power system. The defense worked and Simpson was acquitted.

O.J. went toes up financially, however, in the following civil proceeding in which the Goldman family was awarded $8.5 million for wrongful death.

The Los Angeles cops beat Rodney King senseless on March 3, 1991. The Hollywood Madam, Heidi Fleiss, was brought to trial on September 19, 1994, for running a high-priced call girl operation geared to Hollywood stars and other public figures. The case became famous because it had celebrities and nonviolent undercover work by the cops.

Hey, the crime rate began to decline in 1993.

Do you get leniency if, instead of killing someone because he's gay or a minority, you whack him for the twenty bucks in his pocket?

WHY WE HAVEN'T SEEN GUN VIOLENCE IN PAROCHIAL SCHOOLS

After the tragedy at Columbine High School in 1999, there was a national crackdown on gun violence in schools. Judging by the mail I received, many priests and nuns were not amused.

Timothy James McVeigh was convicted and executed for the April 19, 1995, bombing of the Alfred P. Murrah Federal Building in Oklahoma City. He killed 168 people. His accomplice, Terry Nichols, was sentenced to life in prison on a conspiracy conviction.

The government determined it to be a lone act of terrorism on McVeigh's part. He was angry about the Branch Davidian affair in Waco, Texas, and was generally angry about federal power and perceived threats to the U.S. Constitution, especially to the Second Amendment.

From the moment of the explosion, media and public attention focused on terrorist groups, first foreign, but then domestic. Right-wing militia groups especially came under scrutiny because McVeigh had contact with militia types when he lived in Kingman, Arizona, and shared many of their beliefs.

There was a public backlash against these groups. Some of them were religious fundamentalist groups that operated in cells. Many of them were paranoid nut groups who now, because of the public outrage over the gruesome bombing, actually had something to fear from the government.

From 1978 to 1995 Theodore Kaczynski, under the pen name Unabomber, mailed sixteen packages containing bombs to scientists, professors, and intellectuals. Three of his parcels produced fatal results. The FBI was unable to find him. In the fall of 1995 he wrote a thirty-five-thousand-word Unabomber Manifesto and sent it to the *New York Times, Washington Post,* and *Penthouse.* Without a bomb. He demanded to be published, and, if only *Penthouse* published the manifesto, he would kill one more person. I've known cartoonists to try this, and it never works. Bob Guccione, the publisher of *Penthouse*, was insulted. He pointed out that *Penthouse* had a greater circulation than the *Times* and the *Post* combined. He sweetened the pot by offering the Unabomber a monthly column if he would stop the killings. He stopped short of a Pet of the Month offer, which, of course, would have exposed the Unabomber.

The FBI convinced the *Post* and the *Times* to publish the whole thing on the premise that such a long piece would give away some hint to his identity. Eventually his own brother turned him in.

Perhaps sensing a new trend in murder journalism, O.J. Simpson rang up the *Times*, while stiffing NBC, for his first post-acquittal interview. He made no death threats.

In an amazing turnabout, Robert McNamara confessed that Vietnam was a mistake. In his book *In Retrospect: The Tragedy and Lessons of Vietnam* he wrote, "We of the Kennedy and Johnson administrations who participated in the decisions on Vietnam acted according to what we thought were the principles and traditions of this nation. We made our decisions in light of those values. Yet we were wrong, terribly wrong. We owe it to future generations to explain why."

Many protesting sixties kids had been counseled by their elders that with age and wisdom they would come to see the truth as the secretary of defense did. And so it came to pass.

Time magazine teamed up with CNN to produce a shocking story that the United States had used Sarin gas on its own defecting troops in Operation Tailwind in Laos in 1970. The story was broadcast on June 7, 1998. First Amendment lawyer Floyd Abrams and *Newsweek*, in separate investigations, found the story to be bogus. *Time* and CNN then admitted the story couldn't be supported by facts and issued apologies. CNN retracted the story on July 1, 1998.

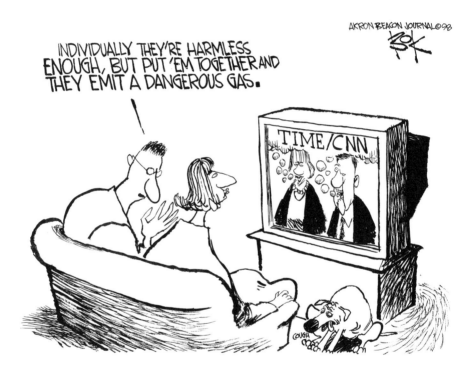

MEET YOUR SECRET ADMIRER.

©95 AKRON BEACON JOURNAL

PBS STRUGGLES TO SURVIVE

The *Jenny Jones Show* raked in ratings dollars on its Secret Admirer segment when the secret admirer of Jonathan Schmitz was revealed as Scott Amedure. The humiliated Schmitz, who said he was heterosexual, later shot and killed Amedure.

After Congress whacked its funding, PBS was looking for ways to spice up its own ratings.

Clinton's first term got off to a rocky start. The day after his inauguration it was learned his nominee for attorney general, Zoe Baird, hired illegal aliens and didn't pay Social Security tax. His next nominee, Kimba Wood, was also shot down, so he had to settle for Janet Reno. Paula Jones sued him for dropping his pants. And on September 26, 1994, Congress killed his legislative pride and joy, Hillary's health care reform plan.

On November 8, 1994, Republicans roared into Congress, led by Newt Gingrich with his "Contract with America." The contract was a gimmick to nationalize the midterm election, and it worked.

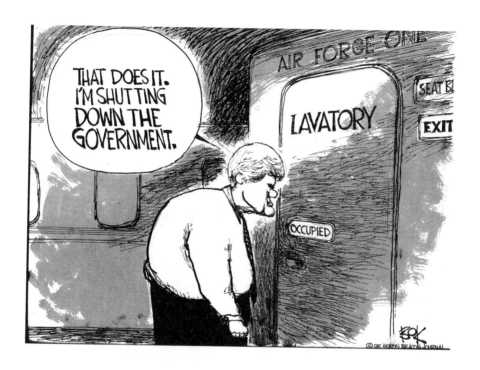

Gingrich passed legislation quickly, enacting large chunks of the "Contract with America" into law. However, he was a Republican mirror image of Clinton. Success went to his head. He was confrontational, he angered people, and he overreached. He threw a hissy fit when Clinton snubbed him on Air Force One. Republicans and Democrats deadlocked over the budget. When the government shutdown came, Gingrich got the blame.

In Congress it is a virtue to appear to succeed when you fail and to appear to fail when you succeed.

The U.S. Senate often moves like a glacier. Apparently it also has the power of a glacier. When President Clinton signed Senate Bill number 927 on March 5, 1998, Lake Champlain was turned into the sixth Great Lake.

As you might expect, the bill's sponsor, Sen. Patrick Leahy (D-Vermont), had greater things in mind than earth, wind, and fire—the U.S. Treasury, for example. The new status allowed Vermont colleges to apply for federal sea grants to study the lake's ecology.

Having seized control of natural forces, the awesome Mr. Leahy sought power over market forces by hauling Bill Gates before the Senate Judiciary Committee to explain why he and his fearsome colleagues should not turn the Microsoft Corporation into a pillar of salt.

Clinton's two terms were a time of peace and prosperity. I'm not sure he caused it, but he didn't hurt it. Republicans say he swept problems like Osama bin Laden under the rug to be dealt with by the next administration. Still, he was in trouble in 1994 when the Gingrich revolution took over Congress. He got a huge break when Newt flamed out.

It's obvious the White House is haunted. What else could explain Hillary Clinton's seeking out psychic Jean Houston to channel the spirit of Eleanor Roosevelt after Nancy Reagan's astrologer consultations? While Hillary was burning rubber on the Ouija board, Bill was triangulating like crazy trying to chart the exact spot between conservatives and liberals that would save him and his party.

There was a beer commercial that made fun of the conniving sensitive male. Two guys are fishing together and one gets all blubbery and says "I love you, man." The other isn't fooled and says, "You're not getting my Bud Light." I choked up as my thoughts turned to my president.

The quirky magazine publisher Steve Forbes ran a Republican primary campaign championing the flat tax with convincing logic. In presidential politics logic is never enough, and his campaign flat-lined.

Bob Dole eventually won the Republican nomination but couldn't seem to get traction in the general campaign. He was reluctant to use his military record against Clinton and unable to engage him on ethics. Clinton moved to the political center and pelted Dole with Gingrich-who-stole-Christmas snowballs, painting him as out of the mainstream. It was rough sledding the rest of the way.

Political consultants identified a new voting bloc they called soccer moms. These were suburban women concerned with issues like education, child care, family leave, and women's rights. Clinton owned them, and Dole couldn't touch them.

With Clinton offering voters the little things they wanted, Dole had difficulty convincing them they wanted government off their backs.

Clinton cast his campaign so wide and shallow that he may have been the only candidate acceptable to everyone at the divisive Republican convention.

With a strong economy and no major foreign policy problems, Clinton skated down the backstretch of the 1996 campaign. The midterm election gave him a scare and moved him away from sweeping plans like national health-care reform. From now on it would be a presidency of small stuff, but at least he got to keep the job. It was the big stuff lurking on the other side of the finish line—including former Whitewater partner Jim McDougal's potential testimony, or John Huang, the Chinese financial fixer he brought into the White House—that should have worried him.

Buttoned-down, mainframe IBM became the biggest software company in the world when it took over the new economy software developer, Lotus Development Corporation.

Until enough of Microsoft's competitors complained, and contributed, the feds had treated Internet companies with a hands-off attitude.

As 401k plans and other forms of employee stock ownership became more popular during the bubble '90s, workers developed a greater stake in the efficiency of their companies. In some cases this resulted in perverse incentives.

As of 1998, 43.6 percent of the adult population held shares of stock. This gave average people a stake in the economy. Unfortunately, it also gave them a stake in the bubble as technology stocks grew out of control. Fed chairman Alan Greenspan tried to talk down the market's "irrational exuberance," but the bubble burst anyway, and a lot of ordinary folks were not happy.

What's up with antiglobalization people? They showed up in large numbers to protest the World Trade Organization meeting in Seattle.

Corporate ownership could and did change hands at the speed of light, and it often wasn't clear who was left holding the bag, or sponge.

Managed care officially becomes unmanageable.

Pfizer pharmaceutical company received FDA approval for its new erectile dysfunction product, Viagra, in 1998. There were some questions about vision problems. Some men reported a green or blue tint to their vision. Loss of vision was reported in small numbers in later studies. Blinded by the drug's success, however, millions of men felt that the benefits far outweighed the risks. Sales rose quickly and continued to remain firm.

While facing Medicare and Social Security disasters, the Clintons went after tobacco, as with most things, to protect children.

In a famous case of penis amputation, John Bobbitt, the amputee, was acquitted of spousal abuse, and his wife, Lorena, got off on a temporary insanity plea.

It's not easy being a friend of Bill.

Chinese leader Jiang Zemin attended a Washington summit in November 1997. Jiang took time for a photo op in Colonial Williamsburg, where he tried on a tri-cornered hat.

Looking as silly as Deng Xiaoping did in a ten-gallon cowboy hat at a 1979 Texas barbeque, but still more dignified than Mike Dukakis in battle tank headgear, the hat trick turned my focus on his compliant host, Bill Clinton. The Clinton administration permitted the transfer of computer, satellite, and missile technology from the United States to China. The Clinton campaign accepted the transfer of cash from Chinese interests and possibly the Chinese military itself.

The paper where I work, the *Akron Beacon Journal*, won its second Pulitzer Prize in seven years for a study of race relations called *A Question of Color* in 1993. The *Beacon Journal* and other community leaders then developed the Coming Together Project to provide a forum for people to express their feelings, frustrations, and observations about race. It's no surprise that such an ongoing gabfest would attract our gabber in chief (or, our first black president, as he was dubbed by poet Toni Morrison), Bill Clinton.

Clinton and his advisory panel held a Town Meeting in Akron in 1997 to open his National Dialogue on Race. It seemed more like a big television revival than a New England town meeting. The faithful came before Bill the evangelist to confess their sins of racial thoughts, words, and deeds. The only voice of dissent came from Abigail Thernstrom, who blasphemed Clinton's cathedral by making a case against racial preferences.

The paper and community leaders were very proud of the event and covered it with praise and little skepticism. There is another ongoing dialogue in newspapers that is not about race. It's about how far a newspaper should depart from being a skeptical observer to an active player in the community. I felt this situation could use a little more skepticism so I gave Chief Wahoo, the Cleveland Indians mascot, a seat on the Town Meeting panel. Chief Wahoo is a big-nosed grinning caricature of an Indian who appears on the team's baseball caps. Wahoo is shunned by right-thinking people around here, and it is the policy of the paper not to use his image. It makes for an embarrassing situation, considering he is the corporate manifestation of the beloved local major league team. We try not to talk about it. Our position on the Chief is the Anti-Dialogue on Race.

I was reprimanded for the cartoon the next day on the grounds that Wahoo is not to appear in the paper. I knew. That was the whole point.

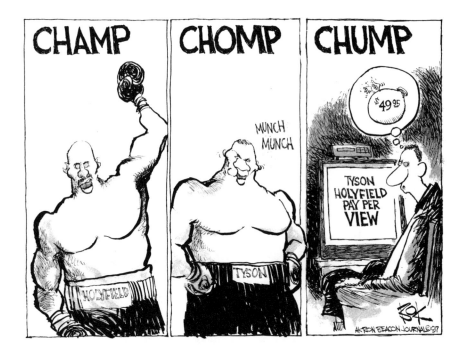

Here's a hard-hitting cartoon with bite.

Evander Holyfield kept his title but lost his ear after being bitten twice by Mike Tyson in a heavyweight title fight at the MGM Grand Hotel and Casino in Las Vegas on June 28, 1997.

A 1988 *Sports Illustrated* story highlighted the issue of out-of-wedlock children of NBA players. That same year Marv Albert returned to his job as announcer with Madison Square Garden Network after an enforced layoff for biting his mistress while wearing women's underwear.

Richie Phillips, the head of the Major League Umpires Association, on July 14, 1999, announced the resignation of fifty-seven of the sixty-six major league umpires effective September 2. Sandy Alderson of the Commissioner's Office called the resignations "either a threat to be ignored or an offer to be accepted." The owners accepted and hired twenty-five minor league umpires on July 22 and 23. Fifteen American League umpires rescinded their resignations, but that left nine American League and thirty-three National League lemmings. The remaining forty-two withdrew their resignations on July 27. The National League, regretfully, had only twenty openings. Twenty-two umps were called out without a strike.

Ever see kids playing ball in a vacant lot? Of course not. No one has time for that.

The Clintons obtained FBI files on 160 Reagan and Bush officials in 1993.

Hillary's billing records from the Rose Law Firm had been subpoenaed by investigators looking into the Whitewater real estate deal. She was unable to produce the records because she said they were lost. They turned up two years later in a book room next to her office.

Clinton could have set goody-two-shoes George Washington straight with the same advice he gave his former girlfriend, Gennifer Flowers.

In reference to questions about their secret affair, Miss Flowers produced a taped phone conversation in which Clinton told her, "If everybody's on record denying it, you've got no problem."

MR. STARR, ANY TRUTH TO THE CLAIM THAT YOU LEAKED INFORMATION TO ME?

AKRON BEACON JOURNAL©08

In 1997 independent counsel Kenneth Starr was being investigated for suspicion of leaking information from the Monica Lewinsky case to members of the press. It was tough getting information out of Starr, so the media would line up outside his house to question him when he carried out the garbage.

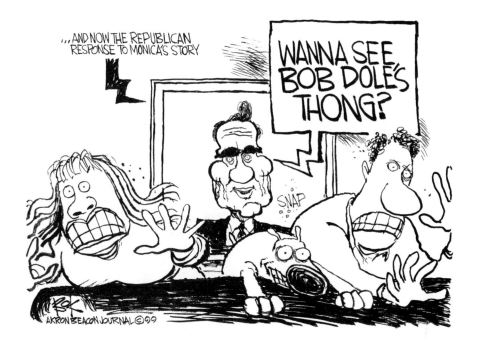

According to the Starr Report, the whole sordid affair began when Monica Lewinsky flashed her thong at Bill Clinton in the Oval Office. People were repulsed yet drawn to this curious information, much as they were fascinated by Bob Dole's public service message that he is a satisfied customer of Viagra for treatment of erectile dysfunction.

Bill Clinton remained defiant while Ken Starr blasted away but could not touch him. Killed in the crossfire, however, was the Independent Counsel Act. Republicans and Democrats had now both been damaged by the act, and they agreed to let it die when it came up for renewal in the Senate in 1999.

KEN STARR'S FAVORITE WEBB SITE

Webb Hubbell, a partner from Hillary Clinton's Rose Law Firm, was named associate attorney general on April 3, 1993. He was a key player in the Clinton move from Little Rock to the White House.

Interest in Clinton's involvement in the Whitewater land deal and the failed Madison Guaranty Savings & Loan (which cost taxpayers more than $50 million in the FSLIC bailout) increased with the suicide of deputy White House counsel Vince Foster, also a Rose Law Firm partner. On November 3, 1993, Hubbell recused himself from the Whitewater case; he resigned as associate AG on March 14, 1994. In June he received a payment of $100,000 from the Clinton-connected Indonesian Lippo Group, as he was being pressured by independent counsel Kenneth Starr to cooperate in the Whitewater investigation. On December 6 Hubbell pleaded guilty to bilking the Rose Law Firm and its clients with overcharges of more than $400,000 and was sentenced to twenty-one months in prison. He agreed to cooperate in the Whitewater investigation and was released after fifteen months.

Hubbell never cooperated. Clinton friends paid him more than $700,000 in suspected hush money, and Starr went after him on income tax charges related to that money. Hubbell pleaded guilty to one charge of income tax evasion.

In the end Starr never could make him talk (Hubbell claims he had nothing to say) and settled the case with a plea bargain and no more jail time in 1999.

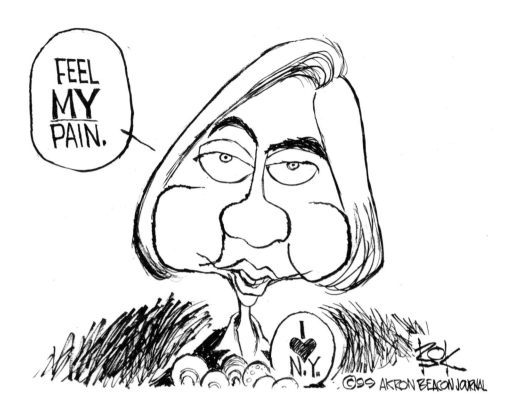

Hillary Clinton stood by her man after all. For all her suffering she earned the right to claim a seat in the U.S. Senate. She chose New York's.

TREASURY SECRETARY RUBIN HANDS OVER THE REINS

Robert Rubin stepped down as Treasury secretary in 1999. His successor was former Harvard professor Larry Summers. Rubin had presided over one of the longest economic expansions and bull markets in history. All that in spite of his crazy cut-up boss.

Not only was the war in Bosnia fought from fifteen thousand feet with no casualties, it was also fought from seven thousand miles away. Bombers took off from Missouri for round-trip missions. It was like an overnight business trip for the fliers. By the way, getting a map off the Internet in 1999 was a novelty.

In 1999 NATO bombers accidentally hit the Chinese Embassy in Belgrade, killing three people. The mistake was blamed on faulty U.S. intelligence. The Chinese, who were alleged to have paid a great deal in the past to steal U.S. intelligence, must have questioned if they had gotten their money's worth.

The Department of Housing and Urban Development prepared lawsuits holding gunmakers responsible for the gun violence in public housing projects. There have been reports of some nongun violence at the public housing project at 1600 Pennsylvania Avenue.

The U.S. policy in 1999 was to intercept Cuban refugees at sea and turn them back to Cuba. There seemed to be a way for baseball players to stay, however.

One of those refugees, Elian Gonzales, escaped from Cuba on a boat with his mother, Elisabeth Brotons Gonzales. The boat sank off the coast of Florida. Elisabeth drowned, but five-year-old Elian was lashed to an inner tube and found by fishermen. Relatives in Miami took him in, but child advocate Attorney General Janet Reno once again acted out with guns and G-men. The INS burst into Elian's home, abducted him, and delivered him to Fidel Castro.

No matter. Elian had been in the United States too long and had already developed a taste for capitalist ways.

ELIAN'S BIG ADVENTURE – THE END

Cast of characters in the Elian saga: Marisleysis, twenty-one-year-old cousin and emotional mother figure to little Elian. Lazaro, Elian's great-uncle and surrogate father figure in Miami. Janet Reno, attorney general of the United States and defender of children at all costs. Infamous novelty cigar aficionado and president of the United States, Bill Clinton. Aging father to his country and everyone in it, Fidel Castro. Donato Dalrymple, the fisherman who plucked Elian from the ocean and started this whole mess. He was also hiding Elian in a closet during the INS raid. The INS agent who plucked Elian from the arms of Donato Dalrymple says the famous A.P. photo showing him pointing his gun at Dalrymple lies. Al Gore showed his independence from Clinton, and hoped to extract a vote or two from Miami Cubans, by proposing citizenship for Elian.

As the stock market soared and the unemployment rate plunged, chairman of the Federal Reserve Alan Greenspan fretted. Mr. Greenspan feared that kind of thing could cause inflation, so he raised interest rates to make everybody feel rotten about the economy and slow it down.

You were a good man, Sparky Schulz. Charles M. Schulz, 1922–2000.

Wilt "The Stilt" Chamberlain, 1936–1999. He was one of the best basketball players ever. In his lifetime he scored 31,419 NBA points officially, and more than 20,000 women, according to his own record keeping.

Reality TV and a craze in kids' reading struck at the same time with the children's mega best-seller, *Harry Potter*.

An HIV-hardened world learned to cope with worldwide computer viruses.

GUILTY | 12
NOT GUILTY | 0
MARGIN FOR ERROR | + OR − 3%

Governor George Ryan of Illinois commuted all death sentences in the state on January 11, 2003, when a study found that thirteen inmates on death row might not be guilty. Some were exonerated by DNA evidence. Ryan had campaigned for office as a pro-death-penalty candidate.

MAN OF THE PEOPLE

During the 2000 election campaign a reporter tripped up George W. Bush by asking him to name the ruler of Pakistan. He couldn't, which put him with 99 percent of Americans at the time.

Playing the famed Expectations Game, the Bush campaign talked their man down, thereby lowering expectations so that when he appeared before potential voters they would be pleasantly surprised.

For George W. Bush a legacy meant a spot in the Yale class of '68. For Clinton it was a desperate struggle to leave something, anything, more lasting than a spot on a blue dress.

Feminist author Naomi Wolf signed on to the 2000 campaign as an advisor to Al Gore. For her $15,000 a month, she dressed him in earth tones and advised that he was a beta male who needed to become an alpha male.

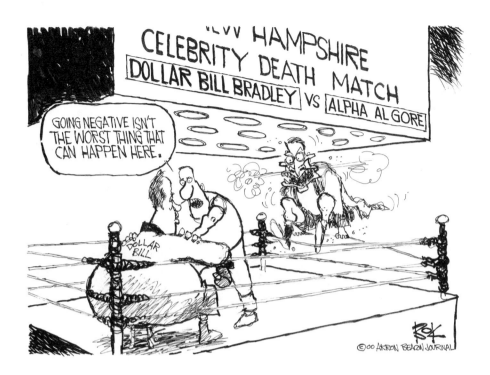

Whatever Naomi Wolf did for her money, Gore came out the angry candidate. He ripped and slashed Bill Bradley in an extremely nasty primary. Bradley, ever the gentleman-scholar-NBA star, mostly took it and lost.

Gore honed his angry-man populist attack on these three corporate interests.

It's true that the major party conventions have become scripted coronations. The World Wrestling Federation, on the other hand, was better scripted than the Reform Party's 2000 convention, which featured Jesse Ventura, Ross Perot, Donald Trump, and Pat Buchanan on the main tag-team ticket.

Buchanan and Ralph Nader, the Green Party candidate, agreed that there's not much difference between Democrats and Republicans. They also agreed that international free trade is bad. Come to think of it, how much difference was there between the Reform and Green parties?

CAN PROTESTERS CLAIM EXECUTIVE PRIVILEGE?

More than four hundred protesters were arrested at the 2000 Republican convention in Philadelphia. Bill Clinton wasn't actually among them, but he did break with tradition by heckling the opposition nominee from the Oval Office.

The major broadcast networks scaled back their wall-to-wall coverage of the 2000 political conventions. Cable networks and dot-coms filled in the gaps.

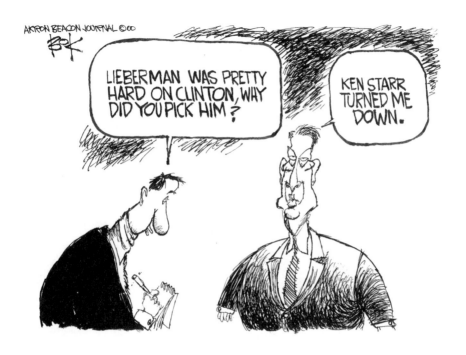

Gore settled on Joe Lieberman as a running mate to further distance himself from Clinton.

The 2000 presidential election turned out to be a statistical tie. Eight news organizations pooled their money and conducted a yearlong study of the controversial Florida results. They found that more people who tried to vote for Gore marked their ballots incorrectly than did Bush voters. So Gore had more voters, but Bush had smarter voters. Thousands of voters in Palm Beach County voted for Gore and Buchanan on the same ballot, while fewer than one hundred voted for Bush and Buchanan. The problem stemmed from trying to cram ten names onto the ballots because of a Florida constitutional amendment that allowed more minority-party candidates. You could say some voters were disenfranchised by having more choices.

SEEKING THE INTENT OF THE FOUNDING FATHERS

SEEKING THE INTENT OF JOE BOB IN BROWARD COUNTY

U.S. SUPREMES

FLORIDA SUPREMES

Ultimately the Florida fiasco was about the intent of the voters, which in a normal place is expressed by a mark on a ballot. Florida voters, however, must be abstract expressionists, because the Florida Supreme Court ordered a recount with special attention to "dimpled ballots" and "hanging chads." From such free-form ballots they hoped to divine the electorate's true intent.

After carefully analyzing all the complex arguments, the U.S. Supreme Court put a stop to the whole thing, thus delivering the election to Bush.

The relentless David Boies, the Democrats' lead attorney, had a mind for detail and amazing endurance.

Bill Clinton survived impeachment and hung on to finish his second term. When you leave a job you usually have to give an exit interview. Clinton gave his to *Esquire* magazine along with a Monica-eye photo pose. He was unrepentant and he harbored more than a trace of bitterness toward his tormentors. He probably wasn't too happy that he wouldn't be attending any inauguration parties either. It would have been different if the ungrateful beta male, Gore, hadn't snubbed him.

After admitting he lied under oath and accepting a five-year suspension of his law license, Bill Clinton's last act in office was to issue 140 pardons. In the most notorious payback pardon since Gerry Ford sprung Richard Nixon, Clinton pardoned fugitive financier Marc Rich, who had been hiding out in Switzerland for the past twenty years. Rich's former wife, Denise, had donated $450,000 to the Clinton library in addition to other campaign contributions. Rich's get-out-of-jail-free card protected him from prosecution for racketeering, fraud, income tax evasion, and illegal oil trading with Iran.

This last act was also the final straw for many of his supporters. The usually reliable Senator Charles E. Schumer (Hillary's future Democratic Senate mate from New York) said, "To my mind, there can be no justification for pardoning a fugitive from justice."

Clinton's closing act as president inspired yet another congressional investigation.

The 43rd president of the United States, George W. Bush, alias: W

CHAPTER 5

George W. Bush

Like his father, George W. Bush used family and money connections to get started in the oil business in Texas. While he wasn't a real baseball player, he did own a share of the Texas Rangers baseball team, again thanks to family connections.

George W. Bush was a political unknown to me when he was elected president. Or appointed by the Supreme Court, depending on your point of view. One thing is for sure: very many Democrats hated him. I didn't know what to make of him. I certainly didn't hate him, but I found it hard to accept the coincidence of the son of a president being elected to the same office, in a country of 240 million. Bush's acceptance speech at the Republican convention, in Philadelphia in 2000, was good. But he was horrible whenever I heard him speak off the cuff.

When the planes hit the World Trade Center towers on September 11, 2001, Bush came into focus. The first impression was his befuddled appearance when he was informed of the attack while reading to schoolchildren. He struggled that first day. But I thought he gave a stirring speech before a joint session of Congress after that. His bullhorn performance with the firemen amid the rubble of the towers was strong. And his first pitch at the World Series in Yankee Stadium was brave and inspiring. I was especially impressed that he threw a strike from the full distance of the pitching rubber.

While he would never have gotten into Yale without his family name, he did graduate and went on to earn a Harvard MBA. His inarticulateness, though, when not speaking from a written script, invited skepticism.

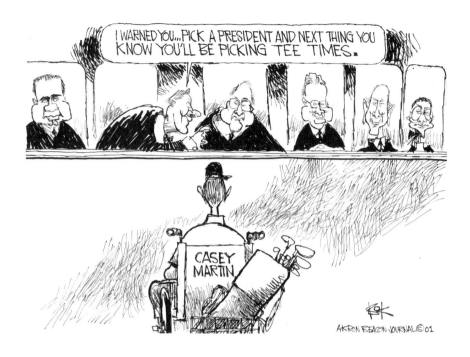

Having freshly minted a new president, the U.S. Supreme Court must have been feeling its oats. The court decided to moonlight by interpreting the Professional Golf Association rulebook. The justices overturned the rule requiring golfers to walk, permitting disabled golfer Casey Martin to ride in a cart.

In a 6–3 decision on June 20, 2002, the Supreme Court ruled that capital punishment for the mentally retarded was cruel and unusual. Would there be an admissions test for the electric chair? Should there be affirmative action for the disabled and low-scoring groups?

Q. WHAT DO YOU CALL A MAN WITH 5 WIVES AND 25 CHILDREN?

A. BIGAMIST

Q. WHAT DO YOU CALL A MAN WITH O WIVES AND 25 CHILDREN?

A. N.B.A. STUD MUFFIN

Tom Green, of Utah, was so responsible he got married five times. At once. If he had fathered his twenty-five children out of wedlock, he would have been within the law. Since no good deed goes unpunished, he went to prison.

On July 18, 2002, the House Ethics Committee recommended that Youngstown, Ohio's, eccentric congressman, Jim Traficant, be expelled from Congress. He later went to prison on a bribery conviction. He was the second person to be kicked out of that body since the Civil War.

The United States was voted off the United Nations Human Rights Commission on May 3, 2001. Members of the commission were a rogues' gallery of nations including Sudan, a country where slavery is practiced.

While Europe battled epidemics of mad cow and hoof and mouth disease, the United States had trouble coming to grips with dead bull market syndrome. The great stock market bubble had burst.

INFAMY II

George W. Bush, after losing the popular vote and finishing the electoral vote in a virtual tie with Al Gore, was having trouble establishing his legitimacy until September 11, 2001. The country rallied and accepted him as commander in chief, and he rose to the occasion by providing decisive leadership. The people of the city of New York, especially the firemen, inspired the whole country and most of the world. Democrats and Republicans rose above politics and pulled together. It was weird.

A measure of America's resilience was that things got back to normal so fast, meaning Democrats were back to hating Bush, Republicans hating Democrats, and much of the world hating America.

The common response to the 9/11 attacks was stunned surprise, but the warnings had all been there. Of course, by the time of the September 11 committee hearings, everyone had seen it coming except the CIA.

Jerry Falwell initially called the attacks God's wrath on America.

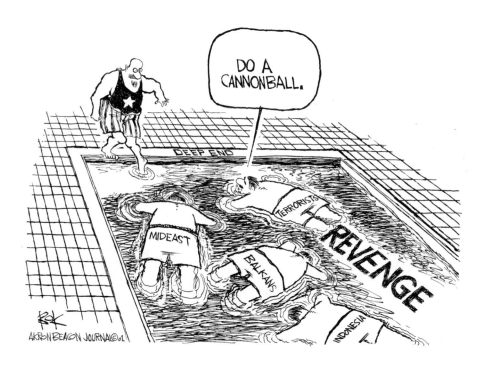

The terrorists wanted us to make a big splash in their pool of death. They eventually got their wish in Iraq.

The war against our enemies lived up to its billing. It proved to be a long, hard, slog. Once again the American attention span was challenged.

OUR AFGHAN WARLORD ALLIES CALL IN BOMBING CO-ORDINATES ON THE ENEMY

The Bush administration should not have been surprised when our allies in Afghanistan seemed interested only in being liberated to attack each other and grab power.

Bush moved on to dessert before finishing the main course.

Some people thought the administration was a little intolerant of criticism.

It is possible to reject our decadent modern culture without waging holy war.

The only thing that could push the war off the front pages would be a sex scandal of Catholic priests. And so it came to pass.

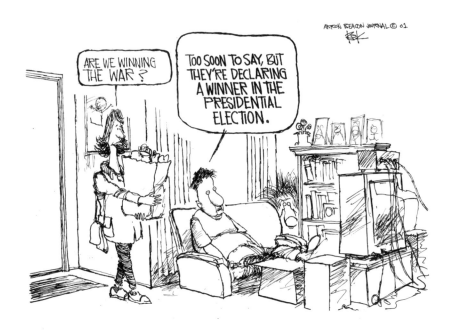

On April 4, 2001, the *Miami Herald* and *USA Today* reported on their joint review of 64,248 Florida ballots. They concluded that if the recount had been allowed to continue, instead of being halted by the U.S.Supreme Court, Bush still would have won. In fact, his margin of victory would have increased to 1,665 votes rather than his certified margin of 537 votes. As Al Gore's luck would have it, they found that counting by the stricter standard the Republicans had wanted, Gore would have won by three votes.

Some Bushies floated the notion that the president didn't need a new congressional resolution to invade Iraq because the last one from Desert Storm was still in effect.

AKRON BEACON JOURNAL ©02

While watching the Super Bowl with his dog, Bush choked on a pretzel and fainted. Whether the dog performed the Heimlich maneuver or CPR is unclear.

Bush advisor Karen Hughes left the White House in the spring of 2002 to spend more time with her family in Texas. She said she would still be in contact with the president by phone.

In testimony before the House Committee on Financial Services on July 17, 2002, Fed chairman Alan Greenspan blamed a breakdown of corporate ethics on a climate of infectious greed.

Enron stock went from $90 per share in December 2000 to zero in December 2001 thanks to the "infectious greed" of its officers.

MR. AND MRS. ARTHUR ANDERSEN

Most people want to show the IRS less money, not more. That's the way it is in the mundane world of individual greed I occupy, anyway. In the go-go world of corporate "infectious greed," money men report cash that isn't there.

You have to live here if you want to make stupid jokes about the Cuyahoga River catching on fire.

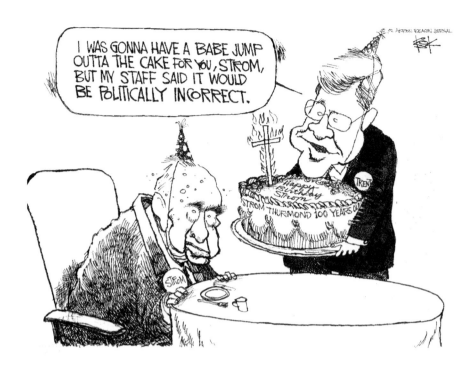

In a toast to Strom Thurmond, Trent Lott told him the country would be better off if he had won the presidency in 1948. Politically correct jaws dropped in unison because Thurmond ran on a segregationist ticket that year, something he had long since renounced.

Gerhard Schröder won reelection as chancellor of Germany in 2002 by running a hard anti-Bush campaign. He was the European leader most opposed to war in Iraq. An al Qaeda cell instrumental in the 9/11 attack operated in the city of Hamburg.

6 MORE YEARS

6 MORE YEARS

6 MORE YEARS

SENATOR
PAUL
WELLSTONE

AKRON BEACON JOURNAL ©02

Senator Paul Wellstone was killed in a 2002 plane crash along with his wife and daughter while campaigning for reelection in Minnesota. He was a well-liked liberal Democrat. His funeral turned into a bizarre campaign rally. Ted Kennedy and the Clintons were cheered while Trent Lott and Jesse Ventura were booed out of the place for paying their respects.

The death of George Harrison on November 29, 2001, provided many baby boomers an opportunity for reassessment.

The last word—obituary cartoons are difficult because I try to show some sensitivity without being sappy. Carroll O'Connor, who played Archie Bunker in the hit 1970s TV series *All in the Family*, died in 2001.

Goodnight, David. David Brinkley, July 10, 1920–June 11, 2003.

Herb Brooks, coach of the 1980 Olympic hockey team, died in a car wreck August 19, 2003.

Two great entertainers, Ronald Reagan and Ray Charles, died in June 2004. Reagan's somber state funeral progressed from California to Washington and back. It was full of pageantry and carried live on television. Many thousands turned out to pay their respects personally.

The Republicans behaved like Republicans, orderly and respectful, but in many ways the week was a carefully crafted campaign event for the reelection of George W. Bush and a continuation of the Reagan Revolution.

The Ray Charles funeral was an outburst of music and joy. It featured great musicians including B. B. King, Stevie Wonder, and Willie Nelson. There were no political subplots. Ray and Ronnie both had a magic touch that caused millions of people to love them. It seemed fitting that Reagan, the "Teflon man" for whom everything always seemed to turn out right, would not have to endure eternity listening to harp music.

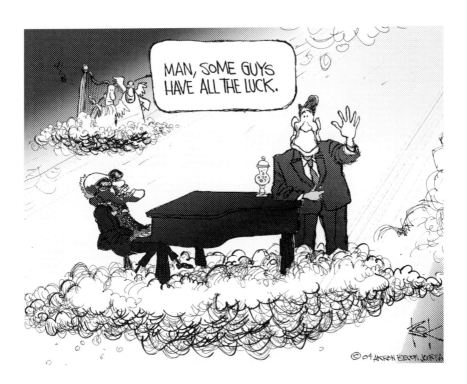

Back in the land of the living, some questioned the legitimacy of the achievements of Mark McGuire, Barry Bonds, and Sammy Sosa.

Major league baseball finally began to take an interest when players were
named in the Balco sports steroids case and Bush commented on the issue in his
2004 State of the Union speech.

When weapons of mass destruction were not found in Iraq, members of the media began to question the president's credibility. Some of them had their own credibility issues, including fake stories by Jayson Blair and Jack Kelley in the *New York Times* and *USA Today,* respectively. Editors at both those papers are gone. The president, for the time, remained.

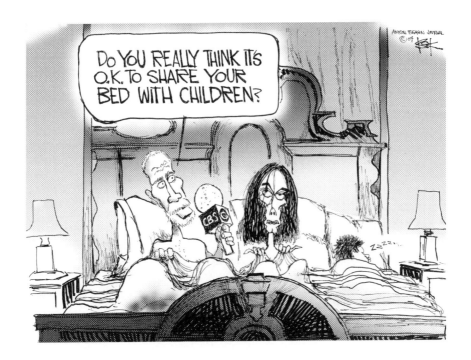

The *New York Times* reported that CBS added an additional $1 million to the license fee it paid Michael Jackson to produce a prime-time special in exchange for Jackson's interview with Ed Bradley on *60 Minutes.* This occurred after the gloved one had been charged with child molestation. Michael Jackson and CBS denied the report.

Terri Schindler-Schiavo was kept alive by a feeding tube, in a vegetative state, for fifteen years. Her husband, Michael, wanted the feeding tube removed. Her parents wanted to keep her alive. By court order the tube was finally removed after an intense legal and political battle, and Terri died at 9 A.M. on 31 March 2005.

Canada, yes, Canada, became a trendsetter. A court of appeal in Ontario struck down Canada's male/female marriage law on June 10, 2003. The theme of gay marriage migrated to the U.S. and became a presidential election campaign issue in 2004.

The more the Supreme Court does the work of politicians, the more it begins to sound like them. In its June 23, 2003, *Grutter v. Bollinger* decision, the court upheld the University of Michigan Law School's affirmative action plan. Sandra Day O'Connor wrote the opinion, saying that a person's race can be taken into consideration as long as it's not done in a "mechanical" way. That means there can't be written formulas.

The court was unable to find a constitutional right to political free speech when it upheld the McCain-Feingold campaign finance law's ban on certain political advertising in the weeks before an election.

DAWN OF THE DEAD

Greenspan the Inflation Killer seemed momentarily caught off guard as commodity prices took off in early 2004.

The earth was shaking over the corporate plundering and stock market shenanigans of the late 1990s. In order to steady the tremors, the corporate chieftains and government bigwigs sacrificed Martha Stewart. She was a big name but a small fish in the financial world. Ms. Stewart had sold shares of ImClone stock just before the price plunged on the revelation that the FDA would not approve ImClone's new cancer drug. Did they get her on insider trading? No. On March 6, 2004, Martha Stewart was found guilty of lying to an investigator.

Alleged right-wing conservative George W. Bush backed and signed, on December 8, the Medicare Prescription Drug Improvement and Modernization Act of 2003. The bill was a huge new entitlement, adding to already exploding medicare expenses.

NATO ALLIES

On the way to the invasion of Iraq, Bush was unable to bring key allies on board, especially the French, Russians, and Germans.

While the United States couldn't convince Saddam Hussein to save himself by complying with U.N. resolutions demanding an accounting for his weapons of mass destruction, Dan Rather managed to land an exclusive interview with the Butcher of Baghdad. Rather's big scoop? Saddam would agree to a televised debate with George Bush.

North Korean leader Kim Jong II seemed to have trouble getting Bush's attention as he focused on war with Iraq. And he actually had weapons of mass destruction.

As U.S. and British forces massed for the battle in Iraq, they were delayed for several days before making their lightning strike on Baghdad. Critics wrote that the military was bogged down, the same thing they said during a brief delay in the Afghanistan war.

As U.S. troops searched for weapons of mass destruction, they uncovered the mass graves of Saddam Hussein's victims.

When Saddam was captured on December 13, 2003, and emerged from his "spider hole," I was reminded of his other frequent pose.

Malaysian prime minister Mahathir Mohamad, in a speech to the Organization of the Islamic Conference, said that Jews rule the world by proxy. No one was heard to object. Leaders of Jordan, Syria, and Pakistan attended the summit. Malaysia is the world's largest moderate Muslim country.

DECISION 2004

TAX AND SPEND

SPEND AND DON'T TAX

As the 2004 presidential campaign kicked off, Bush was proving to be a Reagan-like tax cutter and a Johnson-like domestic spender with a war on his hands.

DEMS SEARCHING FOR CAMPAIGN THEME

The Democrats were unable to take advantage of Bush's weaknesses in the midterm elections. They agreed with Bush's spending, in fact they wanted to spend more, but raising taxes to pay for it would have been political suicide.

Howard Dean let out a now famous scream in a speech following his third-place finish in the Democratic Iowa caucus. Many people suspected his temperament was unstable, and to them (and me) the scream was confirmation. He had built a network of young and equally passionate supporters on the Internet, and raised and spent nearly $50 million. He quit the campaign on February 18, 2004.

While speaking at a Florida Democratic fundraiser on March 8, 2004, Senator Kerry said, "I've met with foreign leaders who can't go out and say this publicly, but, boy, they look at you and say, 'You've got to win this. You've got to beat this guy [President Bush].'" He would not identify the foreign leaders.

Ted Kennedy endorsed his fellow Massachusetts senator early on and tried to guide him in a more vigorous anti-Bush direction.

Kerry adopted the misery index, made famous during the Carter campaign. The only difference was that Carter's misery index was in a time of high interest rates, double-digit inflation, and economic stagnation. Kerry found himself in a growing economy with low interest rates, low inflation, and increasing job growth, so he had to adjust the index.

How did Bob Woodward know everything that went on in the White House? In order to write his book *Plan of Attack*, Woodward must have been in the room serving crumpets while Colin Powell met with Bush to discuss invading Iraq. Powell warned Bush of the difficult postwar responsibilities the United States would face in Iraq. According to Woodward, Powell told Bush, "You break it, you bought it."

U.S. CREDIBILITY, AFTER INVADING IRAQ WITHOUT PROOF OF WEAPONS OF MASS DESTRUCTION ...

DOWN

EUROPEAN ALLIES

WAY UP

LIBYA

While U.S. credibility may have declined in Europe, the opposite seemed true in Libya. Muammar Gadafi came clean on his weapons program and revealed an international nuclear weapons ring.

The plan was for transplanted democracy to flower in Iraq and then pollinate the neighboring kings, sheikhs, mullahs, and thugs. Meanwhile, democratic cross-pollination wasn't taking in the United States' own backyard. Jean-Bertrand Aristide, president of Haiti, courtesy of a U.S.-managed election, was overthrown in a 2004 uprising and shuttled off to Africa by the American military.

AKRON BEACON JOURNAL©04

John Kerry and his supporters said the war on terror called for nuance. The 9/11 Commission was unable to find evidence of an Iraq involvement in the 9/11 attacks. However, there was not much nuance to the message sent by the suicidal maniacs who killed 2,749 people at the World Trade Center, desecrated the corpses of four Americans they murdered in Fallujah, and videotaped the beheadings of *Wall Street Journal* reporter Daniel Pearl and others.

THE SINCEREST FORM OF FLATTERY

A few days after Ted Kennedy said that Iraq is Vietnam, the radical cleric Sheikh Muqtada al-Sadr, holed up in the Imam Ali Mosque, and battling American troops, stole his line.

Al Qaeda operatives blew up three trains in Madrid, Spain, killing two hundred people the week before the 2004 elections. Jose Luis Rodriguez Zapatero, who had been trailing until then, pulled off an upset victory to become prime minister. His campaign pledge was to pull Spanish troops out of Iraq. The election had already been close, but Al Qaeda was quick to claim credit for the swing vote.

In the spring of 2004, Israel tried to end the Palestinian uprising by directly

targeting the Hamas leadership for death. First up was Sheikh Ahmed Yassin.

The frail old man was blown up in his wheelchair by a missile fired from an Israeli

helicopter. The world was distracted from its outrage the next day when a

Palestinian suicide bomber lost his nerve and surrendered. He was somewhere

between twelve and sixteen years of age.

Too bad bin Laden wasn't a Hamas leader. Israel usually gets its man.

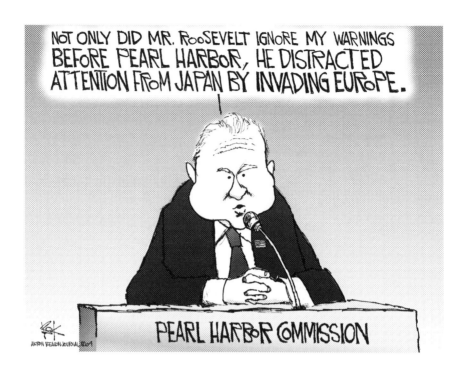

NOT ONLY DID MR. ROOSEVELT IGNORE MY WARNINGS BEFORE PEARL HARBOR, HE DISTRACTED ATTENTION FROM JAPAN BY INVADING EUROPE.

PEARL HARBOR COMMISSION

The star witness at the 9/11 Commission hearing was terrorism "czar" Richard Clarke. In his book *Against All Enemies*, and on the stand, he was appalled that the Bush administration had not acted on all his suggestions. He also considered the war in Iraq a diversion from the real war on terror in Afghanistan.

The Bush administration used outside contractors to provide security in Iraq. The policy backfired when some of them were implicated in the humiliation of prisoners in the Abu Ghraib prison abuse scandal.

FALLUJAH ETHICS

In April 2004, a mob attacked four American security contractors in their vehicle. The mob killed them, burned their bodies, dragged them through the streets, and hung them from a bridge in the Sunni Muslim stronghold of Fallujah, Iraq. Religious leaders objected to the desecration of the bodies as a violation of Islamic Law. There was no word on the moral status of the actual murders.

The Marines vowed to arrest those responsible and bring Fallujah to order. They held the town under siege, but as they were about to finish the job, they were ordered to withdraw, and one of Saddam's former generals was put in charge. Fallujah became a safe haven for Baathists and terrorists, and the war to kill "evil doers" became muddled.

When an Iraqi interim government was presented to the world in June 2004, American networks were almost too obsessed with the Abu Ghraib prison scandal to notice.

In late July, the Democrats held their national convention in Boston. The party's base was strongly antiwar and, with its base in the bag, the leadership was determined to pursue security-conscious voters. Kerry saluted and announced that he was reporting for duty as he began his acceptance speech. He promised to kill terrorists and focused attention on his four months of distinguished service in Vietnam. He must have thought no one would have the bad taste to notice his twenty years of undistinguished service in the U.S. Senate.

Bush bounced to an eleven-point lead in the polls after the Republican National Convention in New York. Kerry was assaulted with attack ads questioning his Vietnam service and got no bounce from his convention.

By the time of the first presidential debate on September 30 in Coral Gables, Florida, Kerry needed a home run to stay in the race. Instead he scored on a passed ball but looked good doing it. Kerry called the invasion of Iraq a colossal error in judgment and stayed on the attack. He demonstrated a command of the issues and looked presidential. The real president, meanwhile, looked as if he'd had a pregame meal of bad sushi.

Advisors warned the president that his father, George H. W. Bush, hurt his chances in his debate with Bill Clinton by frequently looking at his watch. George W. Bush whined that his job was hard, and made faces.

Dick Cheney had better luck in the vice-presidential debate with John Edwards. He accused Edwards of driving up medical costs as a trial attorney. He also accused him of absenteeism. As president of the Senate, Cheney claimed he had never met Edwards. That, of course, wasn't true, but what could Edwards say? "Sure you did, you just don't remember me"?

Kerry claimed he could provide health care, save Social Security, and cut middle-class taxes by raising taxes on the top 1 percent of wage earners.

CBS's *60 Minutes* found itself in hot water again when Dan Rather ran with a story questioning George Bush's National Guard service that appeared to be based on fake documents. As the *Washington Post* broke the story down, Rather stubbornly stood by it. He reminded me of his old stonewalling nemesis, President Nixon.

As November 2 approached, the Democrats assembled armies of lawyers to challenge the armies of Republican workers already assembled to challenge voters in Ohio.

In the final week of the campaign, a *New York Times* story about four hundred tons of missing explosives, believed to have fallen into enemy hands in Iraq, was damaging the president in the polls. Then, in the most bizarre political attack ad ever, Osama bin Laden appeared in a video making the case against Bush. The Evil One (bin Laden) unleashed a litany of complaints, including criticism for U.S. job losses, the size of the U.S. deficit, the behavior of Haliburton Corporation, and Bush for reading a story about a goat to a little girl in the immediate aftermath of the 9/11 attacks. It reminded voters that the enemy lived, and that he hated the president. Just like some Democrats.

On election day the exit polls predicted the battleground states for Kerry. The Kerry campaign became giddy and the Bushies morose. Kerry spokesman Joe Lockhart tried to prevent a Republican legal challenge to his man's projected victory. He said, "There were thousands of lawyers deployed to make sure that no one tried to take unfair advantage, and by and large, it's worked. I've seen very few reports of irregularities."

When the real vote came in, Bush won decisively in Florida. It all came down to Ohio. Around 1 a.m. Tom Brokaw declared the "ground zero state" for Bush. A challenge was unlikely, since Lockhart himself had said the election was fair. Bush won Ohio's 20 electoral votes by a margin of 2.8 million to 2.7 million. The total electoral vote for the country was 286 to 252 and the popular vote, 58.7 million to 55.2 million.

The vast right wing-conspiracy now included Osama bin Laden and the exit polls.

KING OF SWING STATES

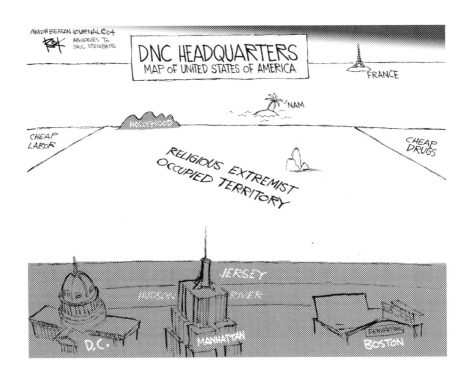

Electoral maps showed Democratic areas in blue and Republican in red. While Bush only managed a 2.7 percent popular vote margin, he carried 83 percent of the geographic area of the United States (not including Alaska, which did not report by county).

Exit polls indicated that moral values were important to Republican voters. These were the same exit polls that misrepresented the early election results, but that was not enough to keep many Democrats from quickly blaming the religious right for their misery. The map in my cartoon represents the Democratic postelection view of the country in 2004.

It's a map that shows two parties, each with no understanding of the other. They are divided by war, culture, and hate for a Republican president. It is to scale. This is where I came in. If I had fallen into a wormhole in 1974 and suddenly appeared in this time and place, I would be lost. I would not be able to get UHF or VHF on the satellite dish. I'd be unable to pump gas with a credit card or get the lights to go off when leaving my car. If you said India, I would think starvation, not outsourcing. I could not order plane tickets online, or lunch by fax, or check my e-mail on a cell phone, whatever that is. I'd have no login or password.

But I would understand the map.